D1611429

# ATLA Monograph Series
## edited by Dr. Kenneth E. Rowe

1. Ronald L. Grimes. *The Divine Imagination: William Blake's Major Prophetic Visions.* 1972.
2. George D. Kelsey. *Social Ethics Among Southern Baptists, 1917-1969.* 1973.
3. Hilda Adam Kring. *The Harmonists: A Folk-Cultural Approach.* 1973.
4. J. Steven O'Malley. *Pilgrimage of Faith: The Legacy of the Otterbeins.* 1973.
5. Charles Edwin Jones. *Perfectionist Persuasion: The Holiness Movement and American Methodism, 1867-1936.* 1974.
6. Donald E. Byrne, Jr. *No Foot of Land: Folklore of American Methodist Itinerants.* 1975.
7. Milton C. Sernett. *Black Religion and American Evangelicalism: White Protestants, Plantation Missions, and the Flowering of Negro Christianity, 1787-1865.* 1975.
8. Eva Fleischner. *Judaism in German Christian Theology Since 1945: Christianity and Israel Considered in Terms of Mission.* 1975.
9. Walter James Lowe. *Mystery & The Unconscious: A Study on the Thought of Paul Ricoeur.* 1977.
10. Norris Magnuson. *Salvation in the Slums: Evangelical Social Welfare Work, 1865-1920.* 1977.
11. William Sherman Minor. *Creativity in Henry Nelson Wieman.* 1977.
12. Thomas Virgil Peterson. *Ham and Japheth: The Mythic World of Whites in the Antebellum South.* 1978.
13. Randall K. Burkett. *Garveyism as a Religious Movement: The Institutionalism of a Black Civil Religion.* 1978.

# HAM AND JAPHETH

## *The Mythic World of Whites in the Antebellum South*

by

Thomas Virgil Peterson

with a Foreword by

William A. Clebsch

*ATLA Monograph Series, No. 12*

The Scarecrow Press, Inc.
and
The American Theological Library Association
Metuchen, N.J. & London
1978

261.2
P442
79072720

Library of Congress Cataloging in Publication Data

Peterson, Thomas Virgil, 1943-
Ham and Japheth.

(ATLA monograph series ; no. 12)
Based on the author's thesis, Stanford, 1975.
Bibliography: p.
Includes index.
1. Ham (Biblical character) 2. Japheth (Biblical character) 3. Southern States--Race relations. 4. Southern States--Religious life and customs. 5. Slavery in the United States. I. Title. II. Series: American Theological Library Association. ATLA monograph series ; no. 12.
BS580.H27P47 261.8'34'4930975 78-15716
ISBN 0-8108-1162-6

Copyright © 1978 by Thomas Virgil Peterson

Manufactured in the United States of America

For my Mother,

HELEN ANN PETERSON,

who has always encouraged my pursuit
of education, supported my goals,
and nurtured my ideals.

TABLE OF CONTENTS

Editor's Note

Preface

Foreword (William A. Clebsch)

I. WEBS OF MEANING IN THE ANTEBELLUM SOUTH 1
- Creating a Unified Culture 2
- A Racial Myth in the Old South 4

II. THE RELIGIOUS WORLD VIEW OF WHITES IN THE ANTEBELLUM SOUTH 12
- The Revelation of God 12
- The Law of God 18
- The Bible as Constitution 20
- The Challenge of Polygenists 24

III. THE STORY OF HAM AND THE SOUTHERN PLANTATION 32
- The Plantation and Bondage 32
- Political Theory and Original Sin 37
- The Curse against Ham 41
- Noah, "The Good Old Patriarch" 48

IV. THE SIN OF HAM AND WHITE RACISM 65
- White Racism 65
- Noah's Curse and the Indelible Mark 70
- Ham's Sin and the Character of his Descendants 74
- The Perpetual Child 79

V. JAPHETH, HAM, AND SHEM IN AMERICA 91
- Japheth's Mission 91
- The Exponents of the Myth 101

VI. THE MYTH OF HAM AMONG WHITE ANTEBELLUM SOUTHERNERS 109
World View, Ethos, and Religious Symbols 110
The Structure of the Ham Myth 117

VII. THE HAM MYTH AS SYMBOL SYSTEM 123
The Nature of Myth 123
Myth and Modernity 132

APPENDIX 141
One Version of the Ham Myth 142

Bibliography 159

Index 177

## EDITOR'S NOTE

Since 1972 the American Theological Library Association has undertaken responsibility for a modest dissertation publishing program in the field of religious studies. Our aim in this monograph series is to publish two dissertations of quality each year at a reasonable cost. Titles are selected from studies, in several different religious and theological disciplines, nominated by graduate school deans or directors of graduate studies in religions in the United States and Canada. We are pleased to publish Thomas V. Peterson's study of the mythic world of whites in the antebellum South as Number 12 in our series.

Thomas Virgil Peterson received his undergraduate degree with distinction at Stanford, studied theology at Harvard, and returned to Stanford where he completed the doctorate in American religious studies in 1975. He currently teaches in the College of Liberal Arts at Alfred University in Alfred, New York.

Kenneth E. Rowe
Series Editor

Drew University Library
Madison, New Jersey 07940

# PREFACE

This book reflects my dual interest in exploring American culture in terms of religion and in understanding the American legacy of white racism. In pursuing these goals I have centered on a white racial myth, prevalent in the antebellum South, that symbolized white Southerners' aspirations and fears insofar as they involved the enslavement of blacks in America. Historians of the Old South have frequently dismissed the white Southerners' use of biblical stories as foolish propaganda. The tale of Noah and his three sons seldom merits more than a footnote in scholarly works that treat the proslavery argument in the antebellum period despite its prominence in writings that defend slavery. Indeed the white Southerners' plantation economy, their racial fears, and their political conservatism are certainly sufficient to explain the entrenchment of slavery in the Old South. The depth of racial prejudice in the United States today will, however, remain obscure unless one seriously grapples with its historical antecedents by examining carefully the white Southerners' notions about slavery and race in terms of their own cultural perceptions. And the myth of Ham and Japheth gave cultural depth to economics, politics, and racism in the Old South.

William A. Clebsch has nurtured this study in all of its stages. As my dissertation advisor at Stanford he provided invaluable suggestions for improving the dissertation's clarity of thought and expression; his enthusiasm for the topic encouraged me when my own interest waned; his rigorous approach to scholarship frequently gave me new levels of insight. I am particularly pleased that he has agreed to write the foreword to this thoroughly revised and reorganized study.

Along with Clebsch, Robert McAfee Brown and Claude M. Simpson, Jr., read various drafts of the dissertation carefully and offered their constructive criticisms promptly.

Frank Reynolds, in 1970 a visiting professor at Stanford from the University of Chicago, guided by initial efforts in applying the category of "myth" to the American context and in formulating the project. H. Shelton Smith and Samuel S. Hill, Jr., suggested initial bibliographic sources.

Hill additionally suggested ways to reorganize the dissertation as a book. Kenneth S. Greenberg and Gary B. Ostrower, two colleagues in the Division of Human Studies at Alfred University who teach American history, critically read the entire manuscript and supported my efforts to revise it for publication.

Ann Polivka, my wife, has consistently encouraged and supported me while I was working on this book. Most valuably she took time from her own very busy schedule as a nurse practitioner to read the nearly final manuscript and to tell me truthfully when sentences and paragraphs needed rewriting.

I am indebted to many others who have critically read parts of various drafts. Amanda Porterfield, David Langston, Mary Wakeman, and Mary Lou Reker offered helpful suggestions. James M. Knox and Florence H. Chu of the Stanford University Library were particularly helpful in tracking down biographical data on obscure Southern preachers and in obtaining rare books through inter-library loan. I also appreciate Mary N. Lane's and Harriet Callahan's efforts to find biographical information in the archives of the Historical Foundation of the Presbyterian and Reformed Churches and the Louisiana State Library. Diane Glover carefully typed the final manuscript. Kenneth Rowe, editor of the American Theological Library Association's Monograph Series, has been very helpful.

I particularly wish to thank the Mabelle McLeod Lewis Foundation for financial support during 1973 and 1974. Financial support from the Alfred University Research Foundation helped defray my research expenses during the summer of 1977.

Thomas V. Peterson
Alfred University
Alfred, New York

## FOREWORD

by William A. Clebsch

By selecting Thomas V. Peterson's book for publication, the American Theological Library Association is maintaining and enriching the distinguished series of recast, revised, doctoral dissertations that the Association has thoughtfully undertaken to make handily and inexpensively available. By inviting me to introduce this book, Peterson has caused me to reconsider what I learned earlier from him through reading several versions of the dissertation in progress and finally (he will forgive the adverb) in completed form. Now he presents us with a mature work that historically analyzes a crucial religious phenomenon, a work that describes the functioning of a myth once compact, then highly differentiated, then powerfully and demonically recompacted. The book in this form makes me applaud both the American Theological Library Association and Peterson. It also says something about the wisdom of rethinking and rewriting dissertations before publishing them. So far, so good.

Further, even better! Peterson's book affirms, in tones and cadences that are measured, sober, subtle, and plain, the salient grounding, in an ancient Semitic tale, of racism among antebellum, Southern Americans. It tells how a people made myth into mischief--that is, how a people made what *we* call myth into what *we* call mischief. Sensitive to how *we* see both things, Peterson also tells how *they* legitimized a legend, and by no means (as we may want to believe) by mere legerdemain. In fact, *they* became enchanted with the sacral power of a story that told them who whites were and that blacks were lesser beings. *They* made a divine decree sanction human discrimination.

It is a delicate duty of scholars to study prejudice free from prejudice. In this instance that duty translates into studying religion free from religiosity. The book wends its way, at once warily and wisely, through rival theories of myths as structural, cultural, and literary entities. It proposes (to me, convincingly) that one need not deny those designations in order to show that this myth (and maybe others) was most importantly religious. Peterson does not pretend to an interpretation of myths that offsets or displaces those of Geertz, Ricoeur, Janeway, Malinowski, Eliade, Lévi-Strauss, Voegelin, and the rest whose heuristics he has learned. He merely shows that the myth of Ham and Japheth in the consciousness of antebellum, Southern Americans did what these theorists think or thought myths do--and much more.

The relation between religiousness and racism has changed radically from time to time and from place to place, from people to people, and from deity to deity. For the most part, at least in the recent West, the trends have represented correlations instead of divergencies. It is no mere accident that the Civil War of mid-nineteenth-century America and the Holocaust of mid-twentieth-century Europe at once haunt and fascinate, at once charm and shame, us today. The two episodes share the exaggeration of an attitude that is implicit in the consciousness of modern Westerners. The attitude comes to expression everywhere in colonialism. Its exaggerated forms are more puzzling. Classical notions of being a chosen people come to be assimilated into the modern consciousness as a sense of deserving to have been chosen. Thus anti-black racism in the United States produced slavery, repression, exploitation, degradation. Even more virulently, anti-Semitism in Europe produced degradation, exile, incarceration, incineration.

Slavery, then, is the attitudinal cousin of genocide, and the earliest intuition of blood- or gene-superiority is the parent of both. Both slavery and genocide explicated the Christian-Western assumption of racial-religious election that, ironically, derived from the progenitors of the victims of modern anti-Semitism. It somehow befalls those who are chosen to choose whom to chasten, and the chastisement increases with the reflection that the chasteners are the chosen. Europe's Jews, new to the experience of cultural and (to some extent, after von Humboldt) political emancipation, cast themselves in the role of being persecutable even before they were persecuted. Perhaps more tragically because more innocently, blacks in the antebellum South of the United States were enslaved before the myth that Peterson explains rendered them enslaveable.

In other words, modern Westerners arrogate to themselves operations that their predecessors left to the deity. Whenever any people undertake the deity's operation in judging the nations, somebody must suffer. The infliction of suffering and imputation of inferiority by one people against another has always caused noise--what listeners to old-fashioned radios called "static"--in the inflicters' system of explaining themselves and the world to themselves and to others. To press the electronic metaphor, myths have served as cultural static-suppressors.

The adroit achievement of Peterson is not simply to instantiate this general human situation but also to show in detail how the tale of Ham and Japheth suppressed static in the self-understanding system of antebellum, white, Southern (and not a few Northern) Americans. Basically, then, the myth functioned religiously then and there and for them because it referred cultural dissonance to the divine will. If you will, the myth enabled God's will to silence the clash of racial superiority and inferiority. Thus slavery took on the character of a sacred institution.

Once more, the step from slavery to genocide is short and easy. Moderns face the stark option of whether to commit themselves to human equality or to commit themselves to extermination. That is no liberal opinion but a historial truism, emblazoned by such modern myths as the myth of Ham and Japheth and the myths of Aryan purity.

When this book was a dissertation, Peterson was persuading his readers--as dissertations are supposed to do--to concede that things were thus with us not so long ago. Now he has had the good sense and the skill to tease these facts and their meanings upon our awareness in a way that helps us to encounter what happened back then even while the encounter helps us to a new awareness of ourselves and, indeed, to a new awareness of our own self-awareness. Careful attention to this book brings the ready reward of information about the antebellum South. On reflection, it yields also insight into the way sacrality governs morality--how it did for them and how it may still do for us. Therefore, with no little pride in having been adviser to the dissertation-writer but with vastly more admiration for Peterson's having turned his dissertation into this book, I commend its earnest reading.

---

Dr. Clebsch is professor of religious studies and humanities, Stanford University.

## Chapter I

# WEBS OF MEANING IN THE ANTEBELLUM SOUTH

In the thirty-year period before the Civil War, Southerners, whose fathers and grandfathers had proclaimed the Enlightenment doctrines of natural rights and human equality, constructed a meaningful universe that incorporated and sustained black subordination. In 1852 William Gilmore Simms, a prominent literary figure in the antebellum South, noted the remarkable shift in Southern thinking. He claimed that before 1832 few Southerners justified slavery "except on the score of necessity." Twenty years later Simms found that very few people in the South questioned "their perfect right" to own slaves; they even thought it was "their moral obligation" to keep blacks in bondage. Slavery was an ethical institution, he insisted, because it conformed to the universal truth[1] [see Notes at end of chapter].

For some reason people need to feel that their everyday values and beliefs accord with the nature of the universe. Clifford Geertz remarks that "the drive to make sense out of experience, to give it form and order, is evidently as real and as pressing as the more familiar biological needs."[2] The justification of slavery took place within a cultural context that white Southerners inherited from previous generations, a context that included religious beliefs and values, social customs and attitudes, economic institutions and practices, and political activities and theories. The proponents of slavery revitalized old cultural symbols and constructed newer ones to provide a "meaningful framework for orienting themselves to one another, to the world around them, and to themselves." This book explores the "webs of significance" that white Southerners spun in attempting to relate black bondage to universal truth.[3] It is a study of white culture between 1831 and 1861, focusing on a racial myth that allowed white Southerners to order their experiences into an intelligible and unified culture.

## Creating a Unified Culture

In 1831 whites in some parts of the South still openly questioned both the morality and the economic advantages of slavery. Southerners who believed that the peculiar institution was a financial burden hoped that slavery would one day disappear. Perhaps the manumitted slaves would emigrate to South America or could be colonized in Liberia. The debate before the Virginia legislature in 1831 and 1832 was, however, the last public discussion in the South about emancipation. During the debate the proponents of slavery successfully argued that colonization schemes were impractical. The antislavery societies in the South, whose membership largely sympathized with colonizing emancipated blacks outside the United States, declined sharply after 1829 and disappeared by 1837.

After William Lloyd Garrison founded the American Anti-Slavery Society in 1833 and began flooding the nation with radical abolitionist tracts, Southern political leaders reexamined their peculiar institution and affirmed its fundamental importance for the Southern economy. Southern politicians who had spoken out against enslaving blacks became silent or even supported slavery after they were challenged by the growing abolitionist sentiment in the North. Clergymen in the South who had voiced moral opposition to slavery were soon forced to mute their criticism or leave.

Thomas R. Dew, a professor of history, metaphysics, and political science at the College of William and Mary in Virginia, stood in the 1840's and 50's among the first Southerners to reconcile a defense of slavery with Southerners' ideas about human nature, social values, and universal truth. He explicitly rejected abolitionist arguments based on the Declaration of Independence that all men are created free and equal. Rather, he insisted that people are born with innate physical, intellectual, and temperamental differences. Yet he did not declare unequivocally, as later defenders of slavery were to do, that mental and emotional differences of race were inherent; he maintained only that huge actual differences existed between the two races. They could, therefore, live together peacefully only if order were preserved by slavery. Emancipation would at best be a cruel hoax that would replace the benevolent institution of slavery with far crueler control by community prejudice and state power. For "custom" and "prejudice" between the two races would degrade the blacks "to the condition of slaves" while the law declared them free. The only alternative would be a war that would exterminate one of the races.[4]

Dew, a true conservative, saw society as restraining man's sinful predispositions. Institutions that integrated the interests of two potentially discordant factions by strengthening bonds of mutual affection were the best form of social control. Dew believed that only the patriarchal institution of slavery could create unity between two otherwise antagonistic races. "The relation between master and servant," he remarked, was a "closer tie" than any other, except for the familial relationships between "husband and wife, parent and child, brother and sister." Slavery as an institution fit into a world view where the family was the ideal social unit. According to Dew, just as the institution of marriage controlled the temperamental differences between male and female, so the institution of slavery regulated the differences between black and white.[5]

Dew also recognized that the defense of slavery had to be consistent with Southern society's most deep-seated beliefs about the relationship between man and God revealed in the Bible. He therefore proclaimed that slavery "was established and sanctioned by divine authority, among even the elect of heaven, the favored children of Israel." While this declaration foreshadowed later proslavery arguments, he temporized considerably by admitting that "slavery is against the spirit of Christianity." Nevertheless, nothing in the Bible convicted the master of sin for owning slaves. Although slavery might be inimical to the highest ethic of Christianity, it was morally justified in America when weighed against the alternatives of emancipation and colonization.[6]

Dew was the first writer to express clearly all the principal theories that would adjust the Southern world view to slavery. Other writers had proposed a few of these ideas; Dew's Review of the Debate of the Virginia Legislature of 1831 and 1832, however, brought them together in a comprehensive way. Later proslavery apologists acknowledged Dew's essay as a pioneer work in revealing the Southern "mind." James D. B. De Bow, editor of the influential De Bow's Review, wrote in 1850 that it was one of the four most significant defenses of slavery.[7] Yet, Dew did not fully develop these theories. While his conceptions foreshadowed the world view that would soon unify the South, he hedged by declaring that temperamental and intellectual differences between the races might possibly be environmentally induced. He viewed black slavery as permitted but not mandated by God's law. Later theorists were to develop an ethical defense of slavery based on the full-blown racist assumption that blacks were inherently inferior to whites and therefore must be controlled.

## A Racial Myth in the Old South

Although a defense of slavery based on racist assumptions fit neatly with the conservative theory that authority should be exercised by those best suited to govern, a strain developed in Southern culture over the extent to which blacks could be considered as fully human. On one level, the more that Southern whites could prove that the Negro race was significantly inferior to the Caucasian, the easier they could justify keeping blacks in bondage as chattel. A few ethnologists even declared that blacks originated as a separate species and therefore were not fully human. But Southern Christians reacted strongly against the position of these scientific racists because it did not conform to biblical truth; God had revealed that all people descended from Adam and Eve. If blacks were a separate species, Christians would have no basis for converting them to Christianity since the salvation of sinners was doctrinally rooted in Adam's and Eve's original sin. Even though Southern Christians resisted demoting blacks in theory to a less-than-human status, rarely did they deny that keeping blacks in bondage on the plantation was immoral. Slavery strained Southern culture at least partially because it focused attention on the seeming paradox between the Christian doctrine of the brotherhood of man and the reality of black enslavement.

Traditionally, religious symbols, narrated in myths or enacted in rituals, have helped resolve cultural contradictions. Even in the most stable societies, such as those of the American Indian, tensions occurred. When a drought destroyed the hunting preserves or a son of the chief mysteriously died, the culture was strained. When the biblical views of white Christians conflicted with racist theories, religious symbols helped resolve the social contradiction.

Symbols are religious when they lodge everyday attitudes and mores within a universal frame of reference. Religion conveys profound significance to institutions and values by providing them with "an ultimately valid ontological status," writes Peter Berger, and "by _locating_ them within a sacred and cosmic frame of reference."[8] Analyzing the white Southern culture in its own terms involves, then, unpacking the system of meanings encompassed by the religious symbols that legitimated the people's values and validated their world view. And no story was more symbolically persuasive in resolving certain tensions between white Southerners' racial values and their most fundamental religious beliefs than was the myth of Ham. Southern versions of the Ham myth placed the institution of slavery squarely within the context of divine purpose.

American expressions of the Ham myth were based on the biblical account in Genesis 9:18-27. Noah had three sons, Ham, Shem, and Japheth, from whom the earth was peopled. One day Noah drank too much wine and fell asleep naked inside his tent. Ham, the father of Canaan, saw his father's nakedness and went outside to tell his brothers. Shem and Japheth, looking the other way, covered Noah. Upon waking, Noah "knew what his younger son had done unto him" and said, "Cursed be Canaan; A servant of servants shall he be unto his brethren." Then he added, "Blessed be the Lord God of Shem, And Canaan shall be his servant. God shall enlarge Japheth, And he shall dwell in the tents of Shem; And Canaan shall be his servant."[9]

Abolitionists, intent on demolishing the biblical proslavery arguments, recognized the centrality of Genesis 9 for their opponents. In 1838 Theodore Weld wrote that the "prophecy of Noah is the *vade mecum* of slaveholders, and they never venture abroad without it; it is a pocket-piece for sudden occasion, a keepsake to dote over, a charm to spell-bind opposition, and a magnet to draw around their standard 'whatsoever worketh abomination or maketh a lie.'"[10]

Abolitionists did not fully understand why the Ham story captivated the Southern imagination. While they recognized its prominence in the proslavery arsenal of biblical texts, they never fully understood its symbolic persuasiveness. To be sure, proslavery writers had frequently used the passage in Genesis 9 as one more proof-text in the long series of biblical verses to uphold slavery. For example, when in 1841 Thornton Stringfellow, a Baptist clergyman from Culpepper County, Virginia, first defended his scriptural view of slavery, he cited the passage as "the first recorded language which ever was uttered in relation to slavery" to show that the *institution* was decreed by God. While he suggested that the decree might still be affecting the relationship between Ham and Japheth in America, he suspended final judgment: "Be this as it may, God decreed slavery--and shows in that decree, tokens of good-will to the master." By 1861 Stringfellow was using the Genesis account in a new way to explain that Ham's enslavement to Japheth in America accorded with God's will for the advancement of civilization.[11]

A brief examination of the Northern and Southern exegetical arguments will begin to clarify the difference between the Ham story as myth and the story as a proof-text to justify slavery. Northerners attacked the use of the Genesis text on the rational grounds of biblical criticism. They argued that Noah's curse was prophecy rather than a divine decree and asked whether the prophecy of Christ's death excused those who killed Jesus; they contended that even if the curse was part of a divine decree, the ordinance was a special permission for the Israelites rather than a general dispensation; they challenged tracing the lineage of the black race to Canaan, maintaining that only Canaan, not Ham, was the object of the curse; and they argued that the spirit of Christianity, encapsulated by the Golden Rule, cancelled many of the special dispensations in the Old Testament such as polygamy, divorce, and slavery.[12]

Proslavery writers also joined the argument with the abolitionists in terms of biblical exegesis. They contended that Noah's curse was not mere prediction, but an ordinance of God and that Noah spoke by the inspiration of the Holy Spirit; they held that the decree was not a special dispensation, applying only to the Israelites, since it referred to the future relations among Ham, Shem, and Japheth; a few believed that Canaan concurred in Ham's sin, while others maintained that the Hebrew text was corrupt and that "Ham, the father of Canaan" was the object of the curse; and they argued that both polygamy and divorce had been specifically prohibited by the New Testament, whereas slavery was explicitly sanctioned by Paul in his Epistle to Philemon, and never condemned by Christ.[13]

My intention here is not to discuss the usage of the Bible to promote slavery or antislavery. Nor will I evaluate the merits or abuses of the biblical arguments or enter into minute details of the debate--e.g., whether Old Testament slavery was the same as Southern slavery or whether the Hebrew *ebed* and the Greek *doulos* are better translated as "slave" or "servant." Several contemporary scholars have already made fine contributions in reviewing these questions.[14] The exegetical arguments have two other bearings on this study.

First, Southern biblical exegesis reveals the primacy of Scripture as foundation for the society's institutions, values, and beliefs. On the least refined level the Ham story merely rationalized slavery in a culture under attack by Northern religious leaders and politicians who claimed that slavery was inimical to the Christian moral law and to the American principle of freedom and equality for all. Yet, a common vision of Southerners as the true inheritors of the original colonists' belief in the rule of God abounded; they were the proud conservers of the nation, protecting the republic from the dangerous "isms" that were sweeping the North. Therefore, Southern apologists continually referred to the "biblical constitution," which in their view circumscribed the United States Constitution.

Second, the biblical exegesis illustrates the difference between mythic and logical thought. The arguments summarized above, while not always profound, have been framed in language that is more or less open to rational discussion. While scriptural critiques helped fashion and rationalize the myth itself, these arguments must be logically separated to show how the story of Ham and Noah functioned in the South to synthesize the white society's racist viewpoint and the "patriarchal" institution of slavery with the biblical world view that governmental institutions resulted from man's sinfulness.

The Southern versions of the Ham myth were rooted in the biblical story rather than controlled by it. In the Southern story, Ham and Japheth became archetypes, respectively, for the black and white races in America; the relationship between these two brothers in the myth both validated and provided a model for the whites' treatment of blacks in the antebellum South. To the extent that the blacks' perception of the universe and their values were molded by those of the whites, they, too, may have been influenced by the Ham story as myth. Black clergymen in the North who encouraged emigration to Liberia preached that God's promise to the descendants of Ham in Psalm 68 would soon be fulfilled; an escaped slave who achieved prominence among Connecticut Congregational ministers did acknowledge his race's descent from Ham, while denying that Ham was the object of the curse.[15]

In most versions of the Ham myth Noah's third son, Shem, who was the progenitor of the red race, was only a minor character. Since contact between Indians and whites in the antebellum South was only marginal, the myth did not provide a detailed model for their relations in the same way that it prescribed the proper roles between blacks and whites. Shem was significant, however, in those versions of the myth that related the growth of the American nation in terms of manifest destiny by explaining that the red man's demise was part of the divine will. Once the myth came to symbolize the white Southerners' aspirations for the spiritual and material ascendancy of America, Shem, as the archetype of the red race, became a major actor in the sacred drama that narrated God's plan for the world.

When Ham, Japheth, and Shem became archetypes for the black, white, and red races in America, the story framed white Southerners' beliefs and values within a sacred history and therefore functioned as myth. As myth the story of Ham symbolized the experiences of whites in the antebellum South; it unified their ancestral past with beliefs about the present and hopes for the future; it fused their racial ethos with their biblical world view.

* * *

Many histories of the Old South have described white racial prejudice and related it to the institution of slavery; some have described the patterns of belief in Southern thinking that supported those attitudes and institutions; a few have shown how the Southern "mind" and the Southern ethos mutually supported one another.[16] This book, however, relates the white Southerners' racial ethos to their world view by centering on the Ham myth as a cultural symbol system. The study of a society's myths is important for an analysis of culture, since "culture," in the words of Geertz, "denotes an historically transmitted pattern of meanings embodied in symbols, a system of inherited conceptions expressed in symbolic forms by means of which men communicate, perpetuate, and develop their knowledge about and attitudes towards life."[17]

NOTES

[1]William Gilmore Simms, Introduction to "The Morals of Slavery," The Pro-Slavery Argument (1852; rpt. New York: Negro Universities Press, 1968), p. 179. See also George Fitzhugh, "Southern Thought," De Bow's Review 23 (Oct. 1857), 341.

[2]Clifford Geertz, The Interpretation of Cultures (New York: Basic Books, 1973), p. 140.

[3]The metaphor and quotation are from Geertz, pp. 5, 250; see also pp. 14, 89.

[4]Thomas Roderick Dew, "Professor Dew on Slavery," Pro-Slavery Argument, pp. 436, 459-60, and passim.

[5]Dew, pp. 456-57.

[6]Dew, pp. 295, 451, and passim.

[7]De Bow declared that the other most important works were the "Memoir" of Chancellor Harper, the letters of Hammond, and the letter of John Calhoun to Mr. King, in Editorial Introduction to "Harper's Memoir on Slavery," De Bow's Review 7 (March 1850), 232. A. J. Roane declared Dew's Review to be seminal in expressing the Southern mind, in "Reply to Abolition Objections to Slavery," De Bow's Review 20 (June 1856), 645. Harper also acknowledged its primacy: William Harper, "Harper on Slavery," Pro-Slavery Argument, pp. 2-3.

[8]Peter L. Berger, The Sacred Canopy (1967; New York: Doubleday Anchor, 1969), p. 33; see also pp. 25, 32.

[9]The biblical quotations are from the Authorized (King James) Version, which was the one most widely quoted by writers on the Ham myth in the antebellum South.

[10]Theodore Dwight Weld, The Bible against Slavery, 3rd ed. (New York: American Anti-Slavery Society, 1838), p. 46.

[11]Thornton Stringfellow, Scriptural and Statistical Views in Favor of Slavery (1841; 4th ed., Richmond: J. W. Randolph, 1856), pp. 8-9. Stringfellow's later work is Slavery (New York: J. F. Trow, 1861).

[12]Examples include Weld, pp. 45-47; William Ellery Channing, "Slavery," The Works (Boston: American Unitarian Association, 1878), pp. 688-743; Francis Wayland, The Elements of Moral Science (Boston: Gould and Lincoln, 1870), pp. 191-235; John Rankin, Letters on American Slavery (1837; rpt. Westport, Conn.: Negro Universities Press, 1970), pp. 80-82; James W. C. Pennington, A Text Book of

the Origin and History & c. & c. of the Colored People (Hartford, Conn.: L. Skinner, 1841), pp. 9-13.

[13]Examples include Josiah Priest, Slavery (Albany, N.Y.: C. Van Benthuysen, 1843), pp. 81-83; James A. Sloan, The Great Question Answered (Memphis: Hutton, Gallaway, 1857), pp. 68, 85-87; Frederick Dalcho, Practical Considerations Founded on the Scriptures (Charleston: A. E. Miller, 1823), pp. 9-18; Nathan Lord, A Northern Presbyter's Second Letter (Boston: Little, Brown, 1855), pp. 42-53; Robert L. Dabney, A Defense of Virginia (1867; rpt. New York; Negro Universities Press, 1969), pp. 101-4; Alexander McCaine, Slavery Defended from Scripture (Baltimore: Wm. Wooddy, 1842), p. 5; and Patrick H. Mell, Slavery (Penfield, Ga.: Benj. Brantly, 1844), p. 15.

[14]See particularly Hilrie Shelton Smith, In His Image but ... (Durham, N.C.: Duke University Press, 1972), chs. 2-3; William Sumner Jenkins, Pro-Slavery Thought in the Old South (Chapel Hill: University of North Carolina Press, 1935), ch. 5; I. A. Newby, Jim Crow's Defense (Baton Rouge: Louisiana State University Press, 1965), ch. 3; David Brion Davis, The Problem of Slavery in the Age of Revolution 1770-1823 (Ithaca, N.Y.: Cornell University Press, 1975), ch. 11.

[15]See pp. 46-47, 96, below.

[16]Eugene Genovese is particularly sensitive to the religious symbols that enabled blacks in the antebellum South to understand their world, to find meaningful relationships among each other, and to survive the economic exploitation of whites. See Roll Jordan Roll: The World the Slaves Made (1972; New York: Random House Vintage Books, 1976).

The first section of Genovese's book and Clement Eaton, The Mind of the Old South (Baton Rouge: Louisiana State University Press, 1967) are particularly insightful in describing how the world view of white Southerners supported and was confirmed by their attitudes, beliefs, values, and institutions. Eaton has explored the thoughts and lives of representative people from different socioeconomic backgrounds and in different professions. A more generalized treatment (and a pioneer work on the Southern world view) is Wilbur J. Cash, The Mind of the South (1929; New York: Random House Vintage Books, 1941).

For a more complete bibliography on world view and its relationship to the white Southerners' ethos, see Herbert

J. Doherty, Jr., "The Mind of the Antebellum South," Writing Southern History (Baton Rouge: Louisiana State University Press, 1965).

[17]Geertz, p. 89.

Chapter II

# THE RELIGIOUS WORLD VIEW OF WHITES IN THE ANTEBELLUM SOUTH

The story of Ham came to be a persuasive cultural myth because it justified black bondage in a way that was compatible with the religious convictions of whites in the antebellum South. James D. B. De Bow, the influential editor of De Bow's Review, attempted without much success to legitimize the polygenetic theory of ethnologists that blacks originated as a separate and inferior species. He recognized that if polygenesis were widely accepted, the abolitionists, those "mad dreamers," would "at once be refuted."[1] De Bow and other "scientific" racists, however, found themselves confronting a Christian orthodoxy whose doctrines affirmed that Adam and Eve were the progenitors of all races. What was the nature of this biblical faith that led to the widespread disavowal of racism based on the scientifically respectable theory of polygenesis? What kind of religion could tolerate and even support the institution of slavery? What was the religious world view that allowed the story of Noah and his three sons to function as myth in the antebellum South?

## The Revelation of God

Historians have often contrasted the Puritan settlement in New England and its holy mission of establishing the kingdom of God in America with the economically motivated early Virginians who were concerned with profit. But Perry Miller argues persuasively that the earliest Virginians were as much motivated by the religious impulse as were the Puritans in Massachusetts. He establishes that the mercantile enterprise included the conviction that the early settlers were God's chosen people in America, analogous to the Hebrews in Israel. The early Virginians shared the Puritan beliefs that God acted in history and that men could understand the divine will by studying particular events. Countering earlier historians, Miller shows that the doctrine of divine providence was not simply a polemical justification "to disguise the economic motive," but the rationale that made the settlers' universe intelligible in the first place, and therefore encouraged colonization.[2]

Quoting early Virginia pamphlets, Miller demonstrates that the original colonists believed that God had disclosed the new continent as part of his holy plan. God, the Virginians supposed, was using men's selfish motives for profit to spread the Gospel around the world: "When mankind has been once more united by the merchants, it can be made one in profession by the preachers." The economic endeavor would succeed, therefore, only if the colonists carried the Gospel with them to the new land. Looking for biblical guidance to explain their mission, Virginians, like New Englanders, saw Abraham as their ideal prototype. If the colonists conformed to God's will as they advanced into the wilderness, they like Abraham's posterity would become a mighty nation, dominating other nations economically and enlightening them spiritually.[3]

Yet spokesmen of early Virginia often seemed less concerned with religion than with growing tobacco. Miller writes that "The leaders of Jamestown were not 'saints' as were Bradford and Winthrop." Still, the mercantile interests were not seen as incompatible with religion, but were rather the means God was using to further Christianity. While the Virginians differed from New Englanders in matters of church polity and social organization, they were "recruited from the same type of Englishmen, pious, hardworking, middle-class, accepting literally and solemnly the tenets of Puritanism--original sin, predestination, and election--who could conceive of the society they were erecting in America only within a religious framework."[4]

The economic, social, and political situation in Virginia soon brought disillusionment to both the colonists and their English investors. The Indian uprising and massacre in 1622 effectively ended the missionary efforts. In 1624 the Virginia Company collapsed in financial ruin; the colonists' claim that the Virginia settlement conformed to God's plan was muted. Thus by the time the Puritans in Plymouth began to proclaim that their commonwealth was the New Israel, Virginians "had already gone through the cycle of exploration, religious dedication, disillusionment, and then reconciliation to a world in which making a living was the ultimate reality."[5]

Yet, while the distinctly theological interpretation of Virginia's purpose receded, the colonists continued to perceive their settlement as a novel experiment. In the revolutionary period the Enlightenment rationalism of the founding fathers, particularly those from Virginia, replaced Christian supernaturalism. Although the nature of the new land's mission changed from God's plan of Christianizing the world to man's design of building a society based on liberty and equality, Americans continued to proclaim that their experiment was a novel beacon of light to the rest of the world. In both Virginia and New England, according to William A. Clebsch, "distinctly Christian gardens were planted and cultivated; the southern one bore fruit political and the northern one fruit theological."[6] Thus, contrary to some interpretations, Virginians became leaders in defining the new nation's place in the world because of the religious heritage rather than in spite of it. That Jefferson and others drew upon the philosophy of the Enlightenment rather than Christianity can, in part, be traced to the Virginians' earlier disillusionment. According to Clebsch, "The Puritan founders of Anglo-America--and the founders of Virginia were in a sense as Puritan as those of Plymouth and Massachusetts Bay--knew that they must subject their errand to the severe test of historical endurance."[7]

Even during the revolutionary period the secular reinterpretation of the nation's religious foundations was by no means universally accepted. It had to contend with the dominant theological vision in New England and the religious convictions of the newer immigrants. In the early nineteenth century the Second Great Awakening undermined rationalist philosophy by converting large numbers to Christ. While it is true, as Clebsch noted, that by 1820 the revival shifted its concern from America as a whole to Americans as individuals or "from novelty to morality," religious fervor had affected the whole nation.[8]

Through missionary and Bible societies, denominational bonds between the East and the West were established, thereby strengthening feelings of national unity. There was a re-emphasis on the revelation of the Bible, even though that revelation was often filtered through subjective personal experience. Simultaneously, religious enthusiasm, especially in the South, effectively stifled the deists and supernatural rationalists who had been contending that God's law could be discovered by looking at nature alone. In 1841 Thornton Stringfellow, a Baptist preacher in Virginia, noted that while there were 203 Unitarian and 292 Universalist churches in the nation, only eight of them were in the South.[9] One of the last influential rationalists in the South, Thomas Cooper, who had been appointed president of South Carolina College and professor of chemistry in 1819, was forced to resign in 1834. Cooper's appointment to the University of Virginia, strongly supported by Jefferson, had already been thwarted in 1819 because of Cooper's unorthodoxy in matters of religion. He was finally ousted from South Carolina College shortly after he contended that the Pentateuch was not written by Moses, was uninspired, and contained a collection of "absurd and frivolous tales."[10] The revivals, then, helped recast the Southern world view by increasingly grounding it in the Bible.

Yet, why did the revivals in the Deep South avoid the extreme subjectivism that encouraged the formation or expansion of such sects as the Mormons, Shakers, and Millerites in the Border states and the North? Or, why did the society in the Deep South become religiously "fundamentalist" shortly after the Second Great Awakening, while many of their coreligionists to the north flirted with religious utopianism? Unfortunately, little research has explored how religious enthusiasm affected the various regions in different ways. Most historians of the revival, following the model of William Warren Sweet, have used denominational rather than geographical categories to make distinctions.[11]

Although the revivalists used similar techniques and preached out of kindred theological positions, Southerners generally held religious enthusiasm within strict bounds. In the 1840's, Southerners, responding to abolitionist attacks on their moral character, recognized that their society was, in fact, religiously different from that of the North. In 1845 Governor James H. Hammond of South Carolina wrote that the South was free from the "excitability" that was creating new fanatical sects in other parts of the Union. He wrote that "few of the remarkable religious Isms have taken root among us. We have been so irreverent as to laugh at Mormonism and Millerism, which have created such commotions farther North; and modern prophets have no honor in our country. Shakers, Rappists, Dunkers, Socialists, Fourrierists and the like, keep themselves afar off."[12] In order to show that the South was the conserver of the nation's true religious heritage, De Bow, Fitzhugh, and others repeated this charge during the antebellum period.[13]

Hammond was at least partially correct when he

attributed the conservative nature of religion in the South to the institution of slavery. He claimed that slavery made the slaveholders more practical, responsible, and even moral, since they were concerned with supporting and caring for large numbers of people outside their immediate families.[14] Whether or not one accepts Hammond's rationale, the institution of slavery dampened religious enthusiasm in the South. Writing about an earlier period in American history, H. Richard Neibuhr explains how institutions influence religious thought and practice. Religion becomes utopian when people believe that the evils of society are caused by bad institutions, trusting that when those institutions are exchanged for good ones, mankind will become moral. When, on the other hand, people believe that the nature of man is essentially corrupt, they do not seek societal answers to problems of good and evil, but settle for perfecting the individual's moral nature and seek to maintain institutions that control the sinful nature of man.[15] And white Southerners believed that the institution of slavery controlled the sinful predispositions of the black race.[16]

The revivals in the early nineteenth century, especially in the South, were primarily directed toward personal morality, attempting to save individuals from universal damnation. Frederick Douglass, a fugitive slave and one of the most influential black leaders in America, described his hopes and those of his fellow slaves when his miserly master was converted at a Methodist camp meeting in 1833. Disappointed, Douglass noted that while his master "made the greatest professions of piety" and turned his home "literally" into "a house of prayer" where "loud prayers and hymns were heard" morning and evening, yet he continued to starve his slaves. Douglass finally concluded that Master Thomas' "conversion was not to change his relation toward men--at any rate not toward <u>black</u> men--but toward God."[17]

Yet in many parts of the nation, especially outside the Deep South, revivals frequently turned toward institutional reform. Timothy Smith has shown that converts thought society would be perfected when everyone was filled with the Holy Spirit. Many reform movements, such as those dealing with prisons, temperance, and schools, were motivated by the revivals; revivalists hoped that by ameliorating abominable conditions sinners could be brought to God.[18] In the North, revivalists such as Theodore Weld and Albert Barnes began to fight against slavery on these grounds. As they joined forces with other abolitionists, conversion became subordinate to emancipation.

As Northern revivalists increasingly became involved in the antislavery campaign, Southern clergymen began to disavow the religious enthusiasm that threatened the foundations of their society. As an example, before 1837 in the General Assemblies of the Presbyterian Church, the "old school" clergy who objected to revivalism on theological grounds were in a distinct minority to the "new school" who supported the Second Awakening. In 1836 abolitionism had become a burning issue at the General Assembly in Pittsburgh and Southerners found that its most ardent supporters were from the Northern revivalist wing of the denomination. Southerners, for the most part, had not been deeply involved in this theological controversy. The attack on slavery, however, made them suspicious of the "excesses" of revivalism in the North. Between the assemblies of 1836 and 1837 Southerners who desired their church to be free of internal agitation by abolitionists formed an alliance with Northerners who wanted to purge the denomination of the new school churchmen. Thus these two pressure groups united to expel the new school clergy, who formed their own General Assembly and retained the name "Presbyterian."[19]

While the two major denominations in the South, the Baptists and the Methodists, did not disavow the theological underpinning of the revival that all men could be saved if they sincerely humbled themselves before God, and while they continued to use revivalist techniques, the institution of slavery limited religious enthusiasm. Their fervor was largely confined to the conversion of the individual and to personal morality, rather than to social and institutional reform.

In the territory that was to become the center of the cotton kingdom, revivals occurred in a setting where institutions--particulary slavery--were already clearly established. The lower southwestern frontier had a pattern of settlement different from that of Northern and Border states. Simultaneously with the adventurer and the small yeoman farmer, the cotton planter bought up the richest land and took his slaves into the territory. Thus, the frontier settlement began with an established social order imported from the eastern coast. On the other hand, in the North, as well as in Kentucky, revivals generally took place among frontiersmen who had not brought so definite a social order with them. For this reason, utopian religious groups such as the Shakers and Millerites could gain followers in Kentucky where settlers were searching for their social identity, while in Alabama and

Mississippi the revival's fervor was confined to individual morality, since the plantation system already provided a focus for the organization of society.

## The Law of God

Although the institution of slavery dampened revivalistic enthusiasm in the South, the religious fervor reinstated the Bible as the bulwark of religion. The Second Great Awakening outside the South led away from earlier Puritan reliance upon the Bible as the objective criterion by which society should be judged, and led toward the pietistic use of Scripture to encourage and validate God's direct communication with the individual. H. Richard Niebuhr has observed that American Protestantism, while always maintaining the doctrine of the sovereignty of God, has fluctuated between two polar criteria for judging the divine will--the subjective and the objective, or "the testimony of the Holy Spirit" and the Bible as the record of revelation. Niebuhr found that religious groups in various periods emphasized the two criteria in different ways.[20] In the antebellum South an unusual relationship between these two elements developed. The Holy Spirit inspired the individual to find his personal salvation; the Bible expressed God's will for society.

Many historians have noted that while the Baptists and Methodists were numerically dominant in the South, the Presbyterians and Episcopalians exercised significant control over the mind of that region. In 1820 there were more than six times as many Methodists and Baptists as Presbyterians and Episcopalians in the states of Virginia, North Carolina, South Carolina, and Georgia. In the southwestern states on the eve of the Civil War nearly 60 percent of the church members were Baptists and Methodists while only 7 percent were Presbyterian and fewer than 2 percent Episcopalian (23 percent were Catholic, mostly in Louisiana, Missouri, and Kentucky). The revivals drew many converts to the evangelical denominations from the less-educated people in the South, where approximately one-third of the whites were illiterate. Neither Baptists nor Methodists required formal training for their clergy, the laity being unreceptive to and often suspicious of preachers who spoke from the head rather than the heart. The people wanted their ministers to make them feel God's presence.[21]

When abolitionists forced debate on the issue of

slavery, the religious response was spearheaded by the Presbyterians, who were best equipped intellectually to meet the attack. Presbyterians of the "old school" variety were dominant in the lower South, molding the educational system along Calvinist lines. Although they comprised no more than 11 percent of the church members in any Southern state, the two most famous academies (college preparatory schools) in the South were run by Presbyterian ministers--David Caldwell's school in North Carolina, and Moses Waddel's in South Carolina. Waddel's academy was especially significant in training Southern leaders; his students had included John C. Calhoun, senator from South Carolina and Vice President of the United States under Andrew Jackson; George McDuffie, governor of South Carolina; William H. Crawford, United States senator from Georgia and presidential nominee of the regular Democratic Party in 1824; Hugh S. Légare, congressman from South Carolina and Secretary of State under John Tyler; and James L. Petigru, a leading Charleston lawyer and Attorney General of South Carolina.[22]

Presbyterian colleges included Hampden-Sydney and Washington College in Virginia. Although the state nominally regulated the University of North Carolina, the University of Georgia, and the Tennessee colleges, Presbyterian clergymen controlled them in practice. Presbyterians founded Transylvania University in Kentucky; while it soon passed to state control, the Presbyterian influence remained. After the trustees forced rationalist Thomas Cooper to resign the presidency of South Carolina College in 1834, it too became friendly to Calvinist theology, since James Henley Thornwell, a leading proponent of "old school" Presbyterianism, was appointed to succeed him.

Princeton, in New Jersey, was the Northern college most influential over Southern education. Not only were one-third of its students from the South in the years between 1820 and 1850, but most of the professors and presidents of colleges in the antebellum South were Princeton alumni. Charles S. Sydnor has remarked, "If there be such a thing as a Presbyterian type of mind, Southern college boys were brought into close contact with it in the early nineteenth century."[23]

Even if there was no "Presbyterian type of mind," there is abundant evidence that Presbyterians expressed what became a Southern type of mind. Although Presbyterian theology--particularly the doctrine of election, holding that men could do nothing toward their own salvation--differed from the revivalist belief that God would save anyone who sincerely humbled himself, the difference bore mainly on the proper method for attracting church members and on ritual and ecclesiastical practices. For Southern Christians defending slavery, there were few theological differences. All believed that society should conform to the principles revealed by God in the Bible. All believed that God's will was literally revealed in Scripture. All believed that the sinful nature of man precluded creating a perfect society. All believed that many God-given institutions opposed the rationalist doctrines of freedom and equality, because they were ordained to control mankind's natural inclination to evil. Baptists such as John Leadley Dagg, president of Mercer University in Georgia, Thornton Stringfellow, a minister in Virginia, and Patrick H. Mell, vice chancellor of the University of Georgia, and Methodists such as William A. Smith, president of Randolph Macon College in Virginia, Samuel Davies Baldwin, a minister in Tennessee, and Alexander McCaine, a circuit-riding preacher in Virginia, North Carolina, and South Carolina, adopted these Presbyterian positions when writing on slavery in Southern society.[24]

In their personal relationship with God, Southerners strongly believed in the subjective inspiration of the Holy Spirit, using the Bible pietistically; for their social theory and practice they turned to the Bible as charter and bylaws. If the Presbyterians represented the intellect in the South, the Baptists and Methodists represented the heart, and heart and mind were at peace on social issues.

## The Bible as Constitution

In 1846 Alexander Stephens declared in the United States Senate that the morality of the institution of slavery stood on "a basis as firm as the Bible." The senator from Georgia maintained that "until Christianity be overthrown ... the relation between master and slave can never be regarded as an offence against the Divine laws."[25] Stephens, who later became Vice President of the Confederacy, was voicing the belief of many Southerners that slavery was compatible with their biblical constitution.

When Northern clergymen began attacking slavery as sinful, white Southerners naturally examined the Bible in order to support their views. They found explicit sanction from the Old Testament in the Mosaic code of laws regulating the Israelite nation. They could find no explicit condemnation of slavery in the New Testament; rather they read that Paul had sent a runaway slave back to his Christian master. Abolitionists, on the other hand, relied heavily on the "spirit" of the New Testament, quoting particularly the Sermon on the Mount.[26] It soon became apparent to Southerners that they were reading the Bible literally, and they accused the Northern abolitionists of interpreting the Scriptures with preconceived notions derived from purely human reasoning. Robert Lewis Dabney, Virginia's leading Presbyterian theologian, believed that "the teachings of abolitionism are clearly of rationalist origin, of infidel tendency, and only sustained by reckless and licentious perversions of the meaning of the Sacred text." He believed that it was necessary to defend slavery in order to show the "true infidel character" of abolitionists "by proving that the Bible is against them." In _A Defense of Virginia_, written during the Civil War but published after it ended, he continued championing the claim that Southern society, based on true understanding of Scripture, was "the cause of truth and order."[27]

Religious leaders of other denominations in the South were equally disturbed by what they believed was inaccurate interpretation of Scripture by Christian abolitionists. Augustine Verot, the Catholic bishop of Georgia and East Florida, wrote that the misfortune of the republic "lies in the misrepresentation of ignorant and fanatical zealots, who desecrate and pollute the Divine word, speaking in the name of God, although they gainsay all the teachings of God."[28] Political leaders joined clergymen, paying homage to the authority of the Bible for regulating social relationships. Speaking before the United States Senate in 1849, John C. Calhoun argued that "the authority of the Bible" was on the side of the slaveholders. William Harper, a judge and United States senator from South Carolina, contended that human reason was fallible and therefore it was presumptuous to rely upon it "without reference to the designs of a superior intelligence, so far as he has been pleased to indicate them" in revelation. Other Southern political leaders, such as Mayor George D. Shortridge of Montgomery, Judge Thomas R. R. Cobb of Georgia, and Governor James H. Hammond of South Carolina, echoed these sentiments.[29]

In the debates on slavery Southerners became increasingly literal in their use of Scripture, for their arguments were better supported by the Mosaic laws in the Old Testament than by appeal to the "spirit" of Christ in the New

Testament and the ethical development of Christianity. Dabney, for one, felt that abolitionists who demoted the authority of the Old Testament were attacking the revealed word of God. Such heresy revealed "the Socinian origin and rationalistic character of these opinions." Others, like agricultural reformer Solon Robinson, accused the abolitionists of "falsifying" the Bible by straying from "the plain letter and meaning of the revealed word of that being whom they worship." John Fletcher, a Louisiana planter, remarked that "He who rejects or dispels the plain meaning of the Bible, rejects our God, and is an idolater." Southerners, then, not only declared, in the words of James A. Sloan, a Presbyterian minister from Mississippi, that "the Bible, the whole Bible, and nothing but the Bible" contained God's revealed will for regulating society, but they also interpreted that document literally.[30]

When a Northern abolitionist, Albert Barnes, quoting Francis Wayland, declared that "the New Testament would be the greatest curse that ever was inflicted on our race" if it could be shown to uphold slavery, Southerners believed that the biblical arguments against slavery had been defeated, and they protested challenging God's revelation with human reason. Bishop Verot wrote that when "modern fanatics" declared "that if the Bible upholds slavery, the Bible must be amended," they abandoned the Christian faith by uttering such "execrable impieties and blasphemies." Governor Hammond believed that abolitionists had to admit their anti-Christian bias, "repudiating _revelation_," and rush "into the horrors of _natural religion_." He quoted abolitionists who stated, "'If our inquiry turns out in favor of slavery, _it is the Bible that must fall, and not the rights of human nature_.'" Hammond believed that when religious leaders "_deny the Bible, and set up in its place a law of their own making_," he could no longer reason with them since "our religion differs as widely as our manners."[31]

The apologists for slavery considered human reasoning to be unreliable. They believed that if Northerners would only turn to "the language of scripture itself" rather than to "higher moral law" or "conscience" or "inner light," the hostility between the sections would vanish. Southern Christians maintained that there were no eternal principles to validate morality except the record of God's will.[32]

Southerners who used the Scriptures as the criterion for judging all social behavior began to regard the Bible as the divine constitution for the world. The code of laws in the Old Testament, which comprised the religious and political ordinances for the nation of Israel, was the only charter for society that emanated directly from God. National laws might vary from one country to another, depending on historical and environmental differences. Yet, all laws should conform to the constitution that God had revealed to the world. While some of the Old Testament laws had been amended by *explicit* statements in the New Testament (e.g., statements favoring monogamy), slavery had not been altered. Southerners did not believe it rational to suppose that the New Testament would have remained silent on such an important issue as slavery (prevalent in the Roman empire at the time of Christ) if Christ had meant to change the Mosaic dispensation. Southern religious leaders were particularly incensed at William Ellery Channing's suggestion that Christ and St. Paul refused to condemn slavery on the grounds of expediency; an anonymous writer in the *Southern Quarterly Review* asked indignantly, would Jesus "compromise with sin, for the interests of his Religion?"[33]

The legal literalism of interpreting the Bible as the world's divine constitution helped revitalize in the South the colonial Puritans' myth of the state. Southerners again saw the nation, or at least the southern half, as the nearly perfect society, whose mission was to uphold God's civil and religious laws as a beacon of light to the rest of the world. In the words of Samuel Davies Baldwin, a Methodist minister from Tennessee, "Our country is 'true and faithful.' It has *never* enacted a *single law* unauthorized by the Divine constitution; nor have the decisions of our supreme judiciary ever been counter to the revealed legislation of heaven."[34]

Abolitionism, Southerners believed, could thwart the divine plan for America, since it challenged the very basis of God's rule, substituting human reason for biblical revelation. In an editorial essay in the *Central Presbyterian* (1856) Dabney urged the nation to restrain the growing abolitionist movement. He eloquently pleaded that if men remained faithful to the Bible, the American "dream, ... inspired by the spirit of the Prince of Peace," would succeed, "that here a nation was to grow up, on this soil which God had kept till 'the fulness of time was come,' wrapped up in the mysteries of pathless seas, and untainted by the step of civilized despot or organized crime."[35]

In that mission the black man was forced into a subservient role. An Alabamian, writing in De Bow's Review, exclaimed, "Does our Bible teach us that God has cursed and enslaved the race of Ham for his own wise purposes, we do not, therefore, interpose our philanthropy and question the wisdom and justice of God." William Gilmore Simms wrote that "the African seems to have his mission." Unlike the Indian "he does not disappear"; he was "designed as an implement in the hands of civilization always."[36]

## The Challenge by the Polygenists

The presence of the enslaved black race did, however, lead a few Southerners to question the literal accuracy of the biblical account of creation. In the decade before the Civil War, Samuel G. Morton, Josiah Nott, and George Gliddon, comprising the core of the American School of Ethnology, along with Louis Agassiz, the prominent Harvard naturalist, theorized that the different races of man were separate species, independently created in various geographical centers.[37] Southerners who supported slavery were frequently admonished by Northern abolitionists that slavery contravened the "spirit of Christianity" because blacks and whites were brothers, all being descendants of Adam and Eve. Both James D. B. De Bow, editor of De Bow's Review, and William Gilmore Simms, editor of the Southern Quarterly Review, recognizing that the theory of polygenesis would provide a sound, scientific basis for enslaving the black race, provided a forum for the new ethnologists in their influential Southern journals.[38] In an editorial essay in 1850 De Bow noted that it was of great importance to discover whether all people descended from Adam and Eve, or whether the races originated separately as distinct species:

> If the whole race have but a common original, then common systems may be applied to all; and the greatest license is given to the 'latter day' theorists, who would organize the world upon certain uniform bases, and fit the same institutions and laws to every stage and condition of civilization. If, on the contrary, this assumption be false and groundless, these mad dreamers will at once be refuted, and the world discover that parliament and congress are unsuited to the Hottentot and the African.[39]

Popularizers of the new ethnology generally insisted that polygenesis did not undermine the spiritual authority of biblical revelation. De Bow, for example, following the lead of Agassiz, proposed that Genesis was the authentic history of the Caucasian race alone and that all biblical expressions suggesting universality could be considered as "figurative."[40] Only Nott and Gliddon launched a frontal attack on the authenticity of the Pentateuch itself. Approximately one-fourth of Types of Mankind (1854) was devoted to biblical criticism; Gliddon produced historical and exegetical evidence to show that Moses probably did not write the Pentateuch and that the biblical text was completely corrupt through transmission and translation.[41] In earlier lectures Nott declared that Genesis was "so confused, so full of contradictions and repetitions, so erroneous in its chronology, so contradictory to the present state of science, and, in short, so unsustained by historical evidence, both sacred and profane," that it could be regarded only "as a compilation of anonymous fragments of unknown origin."[42]

The response to the ethnologists' assault shows the depth of the Southerners' belief in the literal interpretation of the Bible. Two Presbyterian ministers, William T. Hamilton of Mobile and Thomas Smyth of Charleston, led the theological counterattack.[43] Both Hamilton and Smyth argued that scientific theories about human origins could be based only on speculation and that it was more rational to assume that people were descended from a common pair since both blacks and whites shared the most significant attributes distinguishing humans from animals--namely, language, reason, and moral sentiments. Smyth wrote, "The negro, therefore, is just as sensible of his need of the gospel, just as unwilling to believe and obey the gospel, and just as truly changed and sanctified by it when he is converted, as the white man."[44] When reason was supplemented by revelation, the case against polygenesis was clear, for, in the words of Smyth, "the unity of the races is not found in any one, or in any few passages, but in all its [the Bible's] doctrinal and practical teaching."[45]

The ethnologists, according to their opponents, were not only attacking the Bible as a divine record, but also undermining the whole scheme of Christian salvation; if blacks were not descended from Adam and Eve, then there was no basis for converting them, since doctrinally Christ was the "second Adam" who offered salvation to all members of the fallen race.[46] In rejecting the doctrine of polygenesis as an attack on religious orthodoxy, Southern Christians spurned the only scientific defense of slavery that could have justified enslaving the black race. Instead Southern Christians turned to the story of Ham to legitimize their peculiar institution in a way that was consistent with their biblical constitution.

## NOTES

[1]James D. B. De Bow, "Ethnological Researches--Is the African and Caucasian of Common Origin?" De Bow's Review 9 (Aug. 1850), 243.

[2]Perry Miller, Errand into the Wilderness (New York: Harper Torchbooks, 1956), pp. 100-1, 113-15, and passim.

[3]Miller, pp. 115-22, and passim.

[4]Miller, p. 108.

[5]Miller, p. 139.

[6]William A. Clebsch, From Sacred to Profane America (New York: Harper & Row, 1968), p. 47. In Chapter Two, Clebsch argues that novelty is a significant national characteristic and has its roots in religion, though the religious aspirations became secularized: "Once novelty became a national trait ... man took the glory, leaving to God and religion the accumulation of yesterdays while placing in human hands today and tomorrow" (p. 68).

[7]Clebsch, p. 41.

[8]Clebsch, pp. 60-61.

[9]Thornton Stringfellow, Scriptural and Statistical Views in Favor of Slavery, (1841; 4th ed., Richmond: J. W. Randolph, 1856), p. 112.

[10]Clement Eaton, The Mind of the Old South (Baton Rouge: Louisiana State University Press, 1967), pp. 236, 27-28.

[11]For example, Walter Brownlow Posey's studies of the Second Great Awakening in the Old Southwest contrast the attitudes of the various frontier denominations toward the excitement of the camp meetings and rash of conversions. Posey's books include The Baptist Church in the Lower Mississippi Valley 1776-1845 (Lexington: University of Kentucky

Press, 1957); The Development of Methodism in the Old South-West 1783-1824 (Tuscaloosa, Ala.: Weatherford, 1933); The Presbyterian Church in the Old Southwest 1778-1838 (Richmond: John Knox, 1952); and Frontier Mission: A History of Religion West of the Southern Appalachians to 1861 (Lexington: University of Kentucky Press, 1966).

[12]James Henry Hammond, "Hammond's Letters on Slavery," The Pro-Slavery Argument, p. 117.

[13]George Fitzhugh, "The Counter Current, or Slavery Principle," De Bow's Review 21 (July 1856), 92-93; Garnett, "The South and the Union," De Bow's Review 19 (July 1855), 41-42; De Bow, "The Non-Slaveholders," p. 73; and Stringfellow, p. 112.

[14]Hammond, p. 117.

[15]Helmut Richard Niebuhr, The Kingdom of God in America (1937; New York: Harper Torchbooks, 1959), p. 49.

[16]See chapter 4, below.

[17]Frederick Douglass, Life and Times of Frederick Douglass (1892; New York: Bonanza Books, 1962), pp. 108-9.

[18]Timothy L. Smith, Revivalism and Social Reform (1957; New York: Harper Torchbooks, 1965).

[19]The two churches resulting from the split were distinguished only by the names "new school" and "old school." In 1858 the Southerners of the "new school" disassociated from the Northerners' branch, becoming "The United Synod of the Presbyterian Church." In 1861 the "old school" churches in the South broke away, forming "The Presbyterian Church in the Confederate States of America," with which "The United Synod" merged in 1864. When the Civil War concluded, the Southern Presbyterians changed their name to "The Presbyterian Church in the United States." In 1869 the Northern "old school" and "new school" united as "The Presbyterian Church in the United States of America."

For a more detailed discussion about the impact of slavery on the division between the "old school" and "new school" Presbyterians in 1837, see Hilrie Shelton Smith, In His Image but ... (Durham, N.C.: Duke University, 1972), pp. 77-94.

[20]Niebuhr, pp. 63-65.

[21]Posey, Frontier Mission, pp. 417-21 and passim; Charles S. Sydnor, The Development of Southern Sectionalism 1819-1848, vol. V of A History of the South, ed. W. H. Stephenson and E. M. Coulter (Baton Rouge: Louisiana State University Press, 1948); and Eaton, pp. 204-5.

[22]Sydnor, pp. 58-59; and Eaton, pp. 204-5, 219.

[23]Sydnor, p. 69; see also pp. 64-68.

[24]Stringfellow, Views; Thornton Stringfellow, Slavery (New York: J. F. Trow, 1861); William A. Smith, Lectures on the Philosophy and Practice of Slavery (Nashville: Stevenson and Evans, 1856); Alexander McCaine, Slavery Defended from Scripture (Baltimore: Wm. Wooddy, 1842); Patrick H. Mell, Slavery (Penfield, Ga.: Benj. Brantley, 1844); and John Leadley Dagg, The Elements of Moral Science (1859; rpt. New York: Sheldon, 1860).

[25]Alexander Hamilton Stephens, "Speech on the Wilmot Proviso," Alexander H. Stephens, in Public and Private, ed. Henry Cleveland (Philadelphia: National, 1866), p. 87.

[26]No attempt is made here to analyze the biblical argument in detail. For a clear exposition see H. S. Smith, ch. 3.

[27]Robert Lewis Dabney, A Defense of Virginia (1867; rpt. New York: Negro Universities Press, 1969), pp. 21-22, 25.

[28]Augustin Verot, A Tract for the Times (New Orleans: n.p., 1861), p. 8. Clergy from other denominations expressed a similar position. See, for example, McCaine, pp. 13-16; Stringfellow, Views, p. 78; Mell, p. 9; W. A. Smith, pp. 132-133.

[29]John Caldwell Calhoun, The Works, ed. Richard K. Crallé, 6 vols. (1851-1856; New York: D. Appleton, 1888), IV, 516; Hammond, p. 159; Thomas R. R. Cobb, An Inquiry into the Law of Negro Slavery (1858; rpt. New York: Negro Universities Press, 1968), p. 52; George D. Shortridge, "Mr. Jefferson--The Declaration of Independence and Freedom," De Bow's Review 26 (May 1859), 547-59; and William Harper, "Harper on Slavery," The Pro-Slavery Argument

(1852; rpt. New York: Negro Universities Press, 1968), p. 8.

[30]Dabney, p. 193; Mell, pp. 9, 16-17; James A. Sloan, The Great Question Answered (Memphis: Hutton, Gallaway, 1857), p. 17; John Fletcher, Studies on Slavery (Natchez, Miss.: Jackson Warner, 1852), pp. 17, 222; A. Clarkson, "The Basis of Northern Hostility to the South," De Bow's Review 28 (Jan. 1860), 12; Solon Robinson, "Negro Slavery at the South," De Bow's Review 7 (Sept. 1849), 214; and "Channing's Duty of the Free States," Southern Quarterly Review 2 (1842), 147-48.

[31]Albert Barnes, An Inquiry into the Scriptural Views of Slavery (1857; rpt. New York: Negro Universities Press, 1969), pp. 310, 381; Richard Fuller and Francis Wayland, Domestic Slavery Considered as a Scriptural Institution, 5th ed. (New York: Sheldon Lamport & Blakeman, 1856), p. 84; Verot, p. 8; and Hammond, pp. 109, 159.

[32]Fletcher, pp. 18, 97, 222, 245; Sloan, pp. 13, 48; Mell, p. 9; McCaine, pp. 13-16; Stringfellow, Slavery, p. 52; "Channing's Duty," pp. 148, 152; John England, "Letters to the Hon. John Forsyth, on the Subject of Domestic Slavery," The Works, ed. Ignatius A. Reynolds, 5 vols. (Baltimore: John Murphy, 1849), III, 122; Shortridge, pp. 547-59; A. J. Roane, "Ross on Slavery and Stiles' Modern Reform," De Bow's Review 24 (April 1858), 307; and A Mississippian, "Slavery--The Bible and the 'Three Thousand Parsons,'" De Bow's Review 26 (Jan. 1859), 48-49.

[33]"Channing's Duty," p. 149. See also Clarkson, p. 12; Sloan, pp. 28-30.

[34]Samuel Davies Baldwin, Dominion; or, The Unity and Trinity of the Human Race (Nashville: E. Stevenson and F. A. Owen, 1857), pp. 14-15.

[35]Robert Lewis Dabney, "Christians, Pray for Your Country," Discussions, Vol. II, Evangelical, ed. C. R. Vaughan (Richmond: Presbyterian Committee, 1891), p. 397.

[36]Clarkson, p. 12; William Gilmore Simms, "The Morals of Slavery," Pro-Slavery Argument, p. 270.

[37]Josiah Clark Nott and George R. Gliddon, Types of

Mankind (Philadelphia: Lippincott, Grambo, 1854). Supplementing Nott's and Gliddon's writings on polygenesis were contributions from both Agassiz and Morton.

38 William Stanton, The Leopard's Spots (Chicago: University of Chicago Press, 1960), pp. 155-56.

39 James D. B. De Bow, "Ethnological Researches," p. 243.

40 James D. B. De Bow, "The Earth and Its Indigenous Races," De Bow's Review 23 (July 1857), 71. See also George S. Sawyer, Southern Institutes (1859; rpt. Miami: Mnemosyne, 1969), pp. 164-65; and Josiah Clark Nott, Two Lectures on the Connection between the Biblical and Physical History of Man (1849; rpt. New York: Negro Universities Press, 1969), pp. 53, 58, 135.

41 Nott and Gliddon, Types, pp. 466-653.

42 Nott, Lectures, p. 112.

43 William Thomas Hamilton, The "Friend of Moses" (New York: M. W. Dodd, 1852); Thomas Smyth, The Unity of the Human Races (1851), Complete Works of Rev. Thomas Smyth, D. D., ed. J. William Flinn, 10 vols. (Columbia, S. C.: R. L. Bryan, 1910), VIII. Other Southerners joined Smyth and Hamilton in their defense of Scripture, including George Fitzhugh, Sociology for the South (1854; rpt. New York: Burt Franklin, 1965), p. 95; George Fitzhugh, "Southern Thought," De Bow's Review 23 (Oct. 1857), 347; Matthew Estes, A Defence of Negro Slavery (Montgomery: Press of the "Alabama Journal," 1846), p. 69; Thomas Reed, "The Unity of Mankind," De Bow's Review 30 (April 1861), 409; A. J. Roane, "Moral and Intellectual Diversity of the Races," De Bow's Review 21 (July 1856), 65-66; Frederick Augustus Ross, Slavery Ordained of God (1857; rpt. Miami: Mnemosyne, 1969), pp. 29-30; Dabney, Defense, p. 22; and W. A. Smith, p. 182.

John Bachman, a Lutheran minister in Charleston and an important pre-Darwinian naturalist, led the scientific counterattack in The Doctrine of the Unity of the Human Race (Charleston: C. Canning, 1850).

44 Smyth, p. 147; see also pp. 141, 148, 211-32, 249; and Hamilton, pp. 409, 438-39.

[45]Smyth, p. 77.

[46]Hamilton, p. 417; and Smyth, pp. 104-5, 198.

Chapter III

# THE STORY OF HAM AND THE SOUTHERN PLANTATION

In 1861 Alexander Stephens as the newly-elected Vice President of the Confederacy declared that the "cornerstone" of the new government rested "upon the great truth" that slavery was the "natural and normal condition" of the black race.[1] Stephens and other Southern opinion leaders such as Thomas R. Dew and George Fitzhugh, a Virginia lawyer and well known essayist, were claiming that the peculiar institution was especially suited for governing the black race. Significantly, the Ham story not only legitimized slavery in general, as did many other biblical passages, but it also justified the enslavement of blacks in particular. As Ham became widely identified as the progenitor of the black race, the story symbolically linked the institution of slavery with a conservative theory of government prominent in the antebellum South. How did whites perceive their peculiar institution and its relationship to their notions of governmental authority? How did the story of Noah and his three sons symbolically join Southerners' political ideals to the realities of the plantation?

## The Plantation and Bondage

The rise of plantations in the Southern colonies influenced the distinctiveness of that region more significantly than any other single development. Economically, plantations required a large number of workers; politically, they reinforced their owners' perceptions of themselves as enlightened patriarchs who controlled their wives and children and their indentured servants and slaves. While it is certainly true that the vast majority of white families in the South farmed a modest acreage with the help of only a small number of slaves, if any, it is equally true that owners of the larger plantations usually became the most influential political leaders. Edmund Morgan has shown that even while the Virginia

Company was failing financially, its governors and other officials in the colony were accumulating personal wealth by having the best indentured servants bound to their own tobacco plantations rather than to the company's land.[2] Thus political power yielded economic wealth in the earliest days of the Virginia colony. By the revolutionary period the larger planters naturally became the spokesmen for the South and even the new nation. Planters such as Thomas Jefferson and George Washington were, after all, groomed to administer large plantations with frequently unruly slaves.

Historians have long debated why plantations arose in the South. Tobacco was particulary important in colonial Virginia, Maryland, and North Carolina, rice and indigo in South Carolina and Georgia. The geographic and climatic conditions of the South did, of course, make staple-crop agriculture profitable. There are, however, many other reasons why large plantations arose in the South: individuals often obtained large land grants; the large planter could get credit more easily; the "long fallow" method of cultivating tobacco required planters to hold large areas in reserve; the practice of using indentured servants allowed a large labor supply and laws granted fifty acres to anyone importing an indentured servant or slave; and plantations were also consistent with the Southern political belief that the extended family was an ideal social unit.[3]

It is difficult to differentiate, in many particulars, the way white indentured servants and black slaves were treated in the seventeenth century. Both were punished, often by whipping, for running away and for unreliable service. There are even several cases of white indentured servants who died because their masters beat them too severely and frequently. Neither slaves nor indentured servants could leave the plantation or marry without the master's permission. White indentured servants, however, could legally appeal to the courts to protect themselves against extreme cruelty, and their terms of service were usually limited to between four and seven years. For various reasons the labor force on Southern plantations gradually shifted from white indentured servants to black slaves. By the middle of the eighteenth century black bondage had almost entirely supplanted white servitude. The economic and social reasons for what Winthrop Jordan has called the "unthinking decision" to enslave blacks have been explored by several historians and there is no need to examine the complex issues here.[4]

Between the American Revolution and the 1830's proslavery sentiment in the South varied considerably from one region to another and from one decade to the next. In the upper South tobacco became less profitable after 1800. Since the supply had outpaced demand, the price declined, and the market for lower-grade tobacco evaporated. Planters in Tidewater Virginia increasingly turned to such non-labor-intensive crops as wheat because over-cultivation of tobacco had depleted their land. As the center of the tobacco kingdom shifted westward, smaller farms with only a few slaves, if any, replaced the larger plantations. Low prices for tobacco, impoverished farm lands, and the excess of slaves burdened the planters in eastern Virginia.[5]

Virginia legislators who lived west of the Blue Ridge Mountains expressed concern about the political and economic situation in the eastern part of the state. These legislators argued that Virginia's economic woes could be traced to slavery. They hoped to abolish involuntary servitude before it ruined the state. And Virginians owned-one-fifth of all the slaves in the United States in 1830![6]

The insurrection led by Nat Turner in August 1831 was the catalyst for the debate before the Virginia legislature that Charles S. Sydnor has called "the greatest and most searching discussion of the nature and problem of slavery that was ever held in the South."[7] The universal belief in black inferiority and the impracticality of colonization along with the property interests of the over-represented slave owners doomed all emancipation schemes. Although the House of Delegates voted by 73 to 58 to suspend indefinitely discussion of the abolition of slavery, the acrimonious dispute showed that the people of Virginia were divided on the issue in 1832. Delegates from districts with a large number of slaves were heavily for slavery, while those from the west, representing districts with few slaves, were strongly against the peculiar institution. Only a few slaveholders such as Thomas J. Randolph, Jefferson's grandson, suppressed their economic interests and voted against slavery, believing it to be inimical to the rights of man expressed in the Declaration of Independence.[8]

In Virginia antislavery sentiment waned after the celebrated debate in the House of Delegates: the fear engendered by Turner's insurrection abated; better prices for tobacco eased economic conditions; the increasing sale of surplus slaves to the lower South proved profitable and relieved fears that blacks might someday outnumber whites; faltering plans for colonization discredited the emancipationists; and Virginia moderates feared identification with the newly organized, more radical, abolitionist movement in the North.[9]

While men in the upper South debated whether slavery was socially necessary and economically profitable, there was no dispute wherever cotton was the main staple crop. In 1827 Benjamin Lundy, Quaker editor of The Genius of Universal Emancipation, surveyed the strength of antislavery societies in the nation and found that there were 106 societies in the slave states with 5,150 members, while there were only 24 such organizations with 1,475 members in the free states. The Southern societies, however, were centered in areas where blacks numbered less than one-fourth of the population and were controlled by moderates who favored colonizing emancipated blacks outside the United States. Even in 1827 when considerable antislavery sentiment persisted in the slave states, no antislavery societies existed south of North Carolina and Tennessee. Clergymen in the cotton states who voiced moral opposition to slavery had to mute their criticism or leave.[10]

The invention of the cotton gin by Eli Whitney in 1793 made the cultivation of short-staple cotton profitable, allowing one man to gin 350 pounds per day compared with only one pound by hand. Since cotton required 200 frost-free days from planting to harvest, its cultivation was generally restricted to states of the lower South. Cotton was particularly well-suited to slave labor; overseers easily supervised large gangs of blacks who were cultivating and harvesting this low-growing crop that required little care. Frontiersmen needed only a small investment to begin growing cotton; small farmers could acquire large plantations and many slaves within ten to twenty years. Thus, slavery was economically advantageous to wealthy planters in the lower South, and poorer farmers could realistically dream of becoming rich by moving to the less settled regions of the Southwest.[11]

As cotton cultivation spread westward, eventually into Arkansas and Texas just before the Civil War, the Southern economy became heavily dependent on slavery. The increased demand for slaves in the cotton region allowed the states in the upper South to export their surplus blacks. For example, between 1830 and 1850 Virginia and Kentucky exported 12,000 slaves annually to the lower South. A prime field hand in

1800 brought $400; in 1860, from $1200 to $1800. Although speculation inflated the price just before the Civil War, the increase reflected in large part the economic demand for slaves in the rapidly expanding cotton kingdom.[12]

Slavery, then, was a profitable institution--at least for the larger planters--in most periods and most areas in the antebellum South. In colonial times men who could afford to bring indentured servants to America frequently became wealthy. By the latter part of the seventeenth century when health conditions improved in Virginia and the life expectancy of the early colonists lengthened, investment in slaves who would serve their masters for life became even more profitable.[13] Although men in the upper South frequently lamented the economic burden of slavery in the first three decades of the nineteenth century, Carolinian and Georgian planters who grew cotton and rice clearly believed that it was economically beneficial. After the debate before the Virginia legislature, Virginians rarely questioned the economic viability of slavery; rather the position taken by Dew became normative:

> It is in truth the slave labor in Virginia which gives value to her soil and her habitations; take away this, and you pull down the Atlas that upholds the whole system; eject from the State the whole slave population, and we risk nothing in the prediction that on the day in which it shall be accomplished, the worn soils of Virginia ... will be a 'waste howling wilderness.'[14]

Dew and others not only claimed that slavery was economically advantageous, but they also played upon the fears of the white population in areas of the South that had a large number of blacks. Even though the slaves' overt resistance to slavery in the South was neither as well-organized nor as violent as the successful insurrections on the Caribbean islands, there were enough cases of individual slaves' murdering their masters or overseers and committing arson to make Southerners a bit uneasy. Then, too, whites knew that in each of the first four decades of the nineteenth century, bands of blacks had armed themselves and plotted to overthrow slavery.[15] Increasingly, blacks outnumbered whites in the lower South and eastern Virginia where the climate and terrain made large-scale plantation operations profitable. In 1820 blacks outnumbered whites in South Carolina and Louisiana, and were more than two-fifths of the population in Virginia, Georgia, and Mississippi. Only in Kentucky and Tennessee did blacks represent substantially less than the overall Southern average of one-third of the population.[16]

When Southerners began to realize that colonization would not rid their region of the large black population, only two alternatives remained--slavery or crowds of emancipated blacks among them. In the words of Dew, blacks were "increasing and spreading, 'growing with our growth, and strengthening with our strength,' until they have become intertwined and intertwisted with every fibre of society."[17] In 1836 Calhoun declared what would be the antebellum Southern position on emancipation: "to destroy the existing relations, would be to destroy" Southern "prosperity, and to place the two races in a state of conflict, which must end in the expulsion or extirpation of one or the other."[18] If slavery were abolished, the social and political situation would end in chaos since the "nature" of the black race would prohibit blacks from functioning on terms of equality with whites; proslavery writers raised the specter of emancipated blacks engaged in massacres and barbarism by depicting the situation in Santo Domingo and of idle blacks undertaking crime by documenting the high proportion of Negroes in Northern prisons.[19]

## Political Theory and Original Sin

The arguments that slavery was economically advantageous for both the individual planters and the Southern economy, and that emancipation would lead to chaos and racial warfare did not really address the ethical issues raised by Northern abolitionists. Nor did these arguments satisfy the white Southerner's self-image as the conserver of the nation's religious heritage. Self-interest and fear are, to be sure, frequently the motives for people's actions. People who are religious, however, usually legitimize their institutions and customs on moral grounds by claiming that they accord with divine laws or universal principles of human nature. And white Southerners in the antebellum South claimed both. One should not assume that Southerners who insisted that slavery was a moral institution were insincere. For people usually believe their own arguments, especially when they are in accord with both economic interests and other political and social values--in other words, when they form part of a total world view.

Abolitionists argued that slavery was antithetical to the American vision of equality and liberty and that the natural rights of blacks were being denied in the progressive land of freedom. They continually chided Southerners for denying their political heritage, formulated by Thomas Jefferson in the Declaration of Independence. Kenneth Greenberg persuasively argues that the abolitionists had really misrepresented the revolutionary leaders' notions about liberty and equality; Jefferson had carefully circumscribed these evocative principles with John Locke's theory of reciprocal rights and duties.[20] Be this as it may, antebellum political theorists in the South accepted the abolitionists' radical interpretation of Jefferson's views on liberty and equality and then disassociated themselves from it. In the process they formulated a conservative principle of government.

John C. Calhoun, the influential antebellum senator from South Carolina and perhaps the leading conservative political theorist in the United States, clearly articulated the distance between Southern and Northern political views. He declared that the doctrine that men are free and equal by nature caused anarchy in much of Europe and threatened the destruction of the United States under the guise of abolitionism. Jefferson, in his view, had been led to see black slavery as immoral and unjust because he had been poisoned by the false Enlightenment philosophy. It was erroneous in the first place because it was grounded in assumptions contrary to observation--there were mental, physical, and moral differences among people. In the second place, Calhoun believed that Jefferson's philosophy was based on the incorrect premise that human nature could be deduced from the purely hypothetical "state of nature" where every man was completely equal and absolutely free to make and break social contracts with his fellow man.[21]

Against the contract theory of society, Calhoun contended that everyone is born into a political and social state, subject to the laws of his society. This is the true condition "for which his Creator made him, and the only one in which he can preserve and perfect his race." Likewise, man has "individual affections" or selfish instincts that tend toward anarchy if left unchecked by government, for human nature is filled with "passions of suspicion, jealousy, anger and revenge,--followed by insolence, fraud and cruelty." Thus, there is a dual constitution of man's nature--"the sympathetic or social feelings ... and the individual or direct." While both are necessary for human survival and are "equally of

Divine ordination," man's individual affections have become corrupt. Thus, Calhoun falls into the conservative tradition. He was not a rugged individualist, although he recognized man's individual, selfish instincts. He believed that these instincts should be kept subordinate to the public welfare. It is, therefore, the individual's duty to shun vice and to cultivate virtue.[22]

All people, Calhoun believed, would be tempted to follow their selfish interests if there were no governmental control. The best government, however, is one that maintains the necessary order for the functioning of society without controlling "individual liberty beyond what is necessary to the safety and well-being of society." Governmental power, then, should vary from one country to another and even one situation to another, depending on levels of intelligence and moral virtue of the people involved. Thus, no one is born with an innate right to equality and liberty; rather "liberty is the noble and highest reward bestowed on mental and moral development combined with favorable circumstances." Believing firmly in the inferiority of the black race, Calhoun could then proclaim that Southern slavery was the best system of control to maximize both the peace of society and the happiness of both races.[23]

Calhoun believed that while government is "intended to protect and preserve society," it has "a strong tendency to disorder and abuse of its powers." Therefore, the real genius of the founding fathers was not the Enlightenment's philosophy of the Declaration of Independence, but rather the ratification of a strong constitution to protect the individual against a tyrannical government. Since slavery was established in the colonies when the United States Constitution was ratified, Calhoun and other Southerners argued that the federal government could not infringe on the rights of the slave owner.[24] While Calhoun was a leader in formulating the Southern political theory and was its most articulate interpreter, others held similar views.[25]

Conservative political theories and Christian doctrines mutually supported one another in reflecting the Southern world view.[26] Specifically Calhoun's belief in people's basic selfishness fit particularly well with the Christian doctrine of original sin. According to this doctrine Adam's and Eve's fall resulted in both personal alienation from God and communal hardships, encompassing pain, suffering, and death. Except for utopian perfectionists (and there were few, if any, in the antebellum South), Christians traditionally have believed that Christ's atonement created the possibility of everlasting salvation but did not affect God's general chastisement by means of sickness, wars, diseases, famines, earthquakes, and other calamities. While Southern religious leaders squabbled about the universality of personal redemption--the Baptists and Methodists believing that God would save anyone who confessed his sinfulness in complete humility, and the Presbyterians holding that God would choose the elect--they agreed that sin had "filled the world with woe."[27]

Calhoun's political theory fit best with the Calvinist theology of Presbyterianism in the South. Presbyterians maintained that people could do nothing to eradicate their basic sinful nature. Therefore, society would always be in danger of disintegrating unless social institutions such as churches, families, and local and state governments kept men's selfish instincts in check. For all practical purposes, however, Baptists and Methodists agreed with Calhoun's theories of man, society, and government. While they believed that human depravity could be overcome when Christians converted all people to Christ, they also claimed that mankind's sinful nature needed institutional control until then. Methodist William A. Smith, while maintaining that man had a "vigorous moral nature," suggested that "he is also the subject of a carnal or depraved nature," making government "an actual necessity." The object of government, according to Smith, is "the control of the lower nature of man, and the development of his higher nature." God has ordained certain institutions for particular conditions in order "to preserve him from that annihilation ... which would inevitably follow if there were no government, and to secure him in the enjoyment of the highest amount of this liberty which his condition will allow."[28]

John Leadley Dagg, a Baptist educator in Georgia, contended that Christianity would eventually render the "restraints of civil government unnecessary ... by making all men righteous." However, until all men have been healed by God, removing the medicine of governmental control would kill the patient, society. Just as the sick person is "confined to bed, and dosed with nauseous drugs," mankind is subjected to "imprisonment, capital punishment, war, and involuntary servitude" to eradicate evil. Governmental restraints can be removed only after humanity is cured of sin --and that possibility is far off.[29] Judge Thomas R. R. Cobb of Georgia echoed these sentiments, writing that governmental restraint would be necessary until "the great principles of Christianity [are] perfectly implanted in every heart, so as to control every action."[30]

## The Curse Against Ham

Southern clergymen and political leaders not only applied the doctrine of original sin to all people, but also claimed that men had authority over women because of Eve's sin. For example, James A. Sloan, a Presbyterian minister in Mississippi, wrote that "in consequence of woman's being 'first in transgression' of God's law and tempting him to sin, she has been subject to man's authority and the whole sex is inferior." Calhoun drew upon the creation account and Eve's subordination to Adam to show that the axiom of all men being created free and equal was nonsense.[31]

It is difficult for moderns to accept the sincerity of such reasoning because theories of government nowadays do not rest on biblical sanctions but rather on the consent of the governed. If someone repeated Sloan's and Calhoun's arguments today, critics could properly label them as rear-guard polemics--or even outright propaganda--to keep women from gaining their rights. While some people may still believe that women should be subject to their husbands on account of Eve's sin, it would be a rare jurist that would mention such a precedent in a court of law. Today there are few, if any, serious attempts to base political theory on biblical events. Yet when antebellum Southerners connected Eve's sin with women's subservience, they did so to prove other points rather than to argue for the inferiority of women, which they assumed was a noncontroversial topic. Biblical history commonly served as the basis for political theory in the English-speaking world before the eighteenth century. Even though the revolutionary leaders from the South had drawn upon John Locke's theories of reciprocal duties and rights based on people's free consent when they declared independence from England, antebellum Southerners still claimed that governmental authority derived from God's edicts recorded in the Bible.[32]

Thus Sloan argued that all mankind suffers by God's decree, submitting to a life of toil, misery, hardship, disease, and death on account of the sin of Adam, the father of humanity; women must suffer in childbirth and be ruled by their husbands because of Eve's sin; so too, the black race was doomed to servitude by the sin of their progenitor, Ham.[33] John Leadley Dagg, a Baptist theologian and president of Mercer University in Georgia, declared, "As the sons of Adam are bound to submit patiently to the curse which requires them to earn their bread in the sweat of their face, so the sons of Ham are bound to submit patiently to the curse which has doomed them to bondage."[34] The Catholic bishop of Charleston, John England, who desired the eventual abolition of slavery, wrote that since every Catholic must accept Adam's fall as an essential ingredient in the human condition, he should likewise believe that it "certainly was not then against the divine law for Shem and Japheth to use the service of" the black race since their progenitor had been cursed by God for his sinful conduct.[35]

These assertions imply a re-creation in the family of Noah after the flood. While Adam was the father of the whole human race, Japheth, Shem, and Ham were the progenitors of the white, red, and black races, which "<u>originated</u> in the family of Noah."[36] Josiah Priest, a New York harness-maker, whose works interpreting the American experience in terms of religion and the millennium became very popular for a short period of time, was explicit about this miraculous intervention in Noah's family, differentiating the three primordial races.[37] Maintaining that the original human race was red since the Hebrew word <u>adam</u> translates "one that is red," he believed it necessary to show how Japheth and Ham became white and black, respectively:

> GOD, who made all things, and endowed all animated nature with the strange and unexplained power of propagation, superintended the formation of two of the sons of NOAH, in the womb of their mother, in an extraordinary and <u>supernatural</u> manner, giving to these two children such forms of bodies, constitutions of natures, and complexions of skin as suited his <u>will</u>. Those two sons were JAPHETH and HAM. Japheth He caused to be <u>born</u> white, differing from the color of his parents, <u>while</u> He caused Ham to be born <u>black</u>, a color still farther removed from the red hue of his parents than was white, events and products wholly contrary to nature, in the particular of animal generation, as relates to the <u>human</u> race. It was, therefore, by the miraculous intervention of the Divine power that the <u>black</u> and <u>white</u> man have been produced, equally as much as was the creation

> of the color of the first man, the Creator giving him a complexion, arbitrarily, that pleased the Divine will.[38]

Priest, and almost every Southern writer on the Ham myth, used the current philological argument that Japheth's name implied "whiteness" since it meant "fair," "comely," and "beautiful," while Ham meant "dark," "hot," and "black," thus proving that these men were, in fact, the original ancestors of the white and black races.[39] Thus when Ham came to be identified as the progenitor of the black race, the story not only legitimized slavery in the abstract, but it also justified the enslavement of the black race in particular. It lodged the peculiar institution's origin in a divine edict which sealed the fate of blacks for all time. But when did this identification of Ham as progenitor of the black race arise? And how widespread was it in the antebellum period?

Few exponents of the Ham story cited sources for their arguments. Fortunately, however, a couple of clergymen mentioned Bishop Thomas Newton, who was chaplain to King George II. Newton published *Dissertations on the Prophecies, Which Have Remarkably Been Fulfilled, and at This Time Are Fulfilling in the World* in 1759. The first chapter presents Noah's prophecy to Ham, Japheth, and Shem. Newton insisted that "the *curse* of *servitude*" and "the promise of *blessing* and *inlargement*" extended to the future races. Newton claimed that Noah had given Africa to Ham as his inheritance; he also believed that "the poor negroes ... who are sold and bought like beasts in the market and are conveyed from one quarter of the world to do the work of beasts in another" were fulfilling the ancient prophecy of Noah. He argued that the text of Genesis 9:25 was corrupt and should read "cursed be *Ham* *the* *father* *of* Canaan." The story, Newton argued, would be more coherent and poetically rhythmical in the original Hebrew if Ham were the object of the curse. Indeed, he cited an Arabic version of Genesis that had the complete phrase, "Cursed be Ham the father of Canaan," and he referred to other versions of the Septuagint that only had "Cursed be Ham."[40]

Interestingly, Newton cited Augustin Calmet's *Dictionary of the Holy Bible* to support his contention that some versions of the Bible read simply "Cursed be Ham." Calmet was a French Benedictine abbott of Senones, who originally published the four-volume dictionary in 1722-1728 in Paris.

Calmet translated the name "Ham" as "burnt," "swarthy," and "black" and maintained that Noah had given him Africa for his inheritance. Calmet was not only familiar with traditional Christian sources, but also with legends from non-Christian lands and rabbinical traditions. Drawing upon these, Calmet wrote "that Noah having cursed Ham and Canaan, the effect was, that not only their posterity became subject to their brethren, and was born, as we may say, in slavery, but likewise that the colour of their skin suddenly became black...."[41]

Jewish midrashim (folk stories and legends), collected in the Babylonian Talmud between A.D. 200 and 600 and found in other writings before A.D. 1000, first suggested that blackness and slavery resulted from Noah's curse. These midrashim variously described Ham's sin as filial disrespect, castration, sexual abuse, and illicit sex on the ark. The Jewish legends identified Ham as the father of the Negro race:

> The descendants of Ham ... have red eyes, because Ham looked upon the nakedness of his father; they have misshapen lips, because Ham spoke with his lips to his brothers about the unseemly condition of his father; they have twisted curly hair, because Ham turned and twisted his head round to see the nakedness of his father; and they go about naked, because Ham did not cover the nakedness of his father.[42]

The use of the story of Noah and his three sons to legitimize the enslavement of blacks in America goes back to at least the beginning of the eighteenth century. In 1700 Samuel Sewall, a New England Puritan, presaging later abolitionist writers who attacked proslavery biblical arguments, expressed doubt that blacks could be traced back to Ham; he believed that even if the lineage could be authenticated, there was no evidence that Noah's curse was still in effect.[43] John Woolman, a prominent Quaker abolitionist, contemptously dismissed the argument, which he had encountered in his travels through the South in the mid-eighteenth century, that blacks could be enslaved because they were the descendants of Ham.[44]

After 1830 when the proslavery advocates began justifying the peculiar institution in their battle of words against the abolitionists, Noah's curse became one of the most frequently used arguments to uphold the enslavement of the black race. The proponents of slavery, however, not only identified Ham as black in polemical contexts that justified slavery, but official church reports promoting white missionary activity among blacks referred to the Negro as descended from Ham. For example, in 1859 the Report of the Tennessee Conference of the Methodist Episcopal Church (South) declared that God placed the African in America not only that he might serve the economic necessities of society, but also that he might gain the blessings of Christianity: "'Heaven devolves an immense responsibility upon us with reference to these sable sons of Ham.'"[45] In the same year the South Carolina Conference of this church challenged fellow ministers "'to instruct these children of Ham in the plan of salvation.'"[46]

Politicians helped popularize the identification of the blacks as sons of Ham. As early as 1818 Senator William Smith of South Carolina used the Noah-Ham story in the United States Senate in a speech in favor of a bill for recovering fugitive slaves:

> Ham sinned against his God and against his father, for which, Noah, the inspired patriarch cursed Cana[a]n, the son of Ham.... This very African race are the descendants of Canan, and have been the slaves of various nations, and are still expiating, in bondage, the curse upon themselves and their progenitors.[47]

Later, Alexander H. Stephens delivered his famous "Corner-Stone Speech" before an overflow crowd in Savannah on March 21, 1861, outlining the principles on which the Confederacy was based. He maintained that "Many governments have been founded upon the principle of the subordination and serfdom of certain classes of the same race" although this clearly violated "the ordination of Providence" and "the laws of nature." Implicit in the speech was the recognition that subservience of some sort is the basis for the progress of civilization, echoing the views of other prominent Southerners like Thomas R. Dew, president of the College of William and Mary, and George Fitzhugh, a Virginia lawyer and well-known essayist. The "corner-stone" of the newly formed Confederacy was the constitution's conformity to both the laws of nature and the will of God revealed in the Bible. Therefore, while all white men "however high or low, rich or poor, are equal in the eye of the law," the proper status of the Negro is subordination to white rule: "He, by nature, or by the curse against Canaan, is fitted for that condition which he occupies in our system.... It is, indeed, in conformity with the ordinance of the Creator."[48] Thomas R. R. Cobb, a well-known Georgia judge, wrote in 1858 that it was the "opinion of many" Southerners that "the curse of Ham is now being executed upon his descendants, in the enslavement of the negro race."[49]

Thirty years after the Civil War, Mark Twain used "the curse of Ham" in Pudd'nhead Wilson as the climax to a central passage. While slavery is only one of the themes of the book, the story is in part a satire on the antebellum attitudes toward the subordination of the black race to the white. It is the story of two boys, Chambers and Tom, one born of an affair between a white man and Roxana, a slave woman who was one-sixteenth black, and the other the son of a free man and master of the house. Roxana switched the two in their cribs. The free boy grew up thinking he was a slave and was treated as an inferior by society; the slave boy became the new master. When Tom discovered he was really the son of a slave, his world turned upside down. His past training, including the beliefs that the black man was inferior, made him involuntarily shun shaking hands with former friends, step out of the path of rowdy and less educated white youths, and keep his eyes downcast. Finding himself involuntarily acting in this unusual manner, "He said to himself that the curse of Ham was upon him." The "curse of Ham" added an ironic note since it climaxed a passage, showing that the blacks' feelings of inferiority were environmentally conditioned. Since Twain used it without any explanation, he must have believed that it was part of his readers' cultural vocabulary.[50]

While Northern black preachers strongly disagreed that the curse of Canaan could be applied to blacks in America to justify slavery, many accepted the idea that blacks were, in fact, descendants of Ham. James W. C. Pennington, a leader in the abolitionist movement, was a former slave who had escaped from the South at the age of 21, and had become a Congregational minister, twice serving as president of the Hartford Central Association of Congregational Ministers. In a pamphlet he boldly declared that blacks were indeed descendants of Ham through the amalgamation of two of his sons, Cush and Mizraim. However, he strongly denied any relationship to Canaan, who was the object of the curse. He sarcastically suggested that the slave owners might have a better case if they went out and found the Canaanites and enslaved them.[51]

Other black clergymen maintained that the prophecy in Psalm 68:31 that "Great men will come from Egypt, Ethiopia will stretch out her hands to God" was God's blessing on the race of Ham. Black clergymen preached numerous sermons on this text.[52] For example, Edward W. Blyden, a black Presbyterian minister who later emigrated to Liberia to become president of Liberia College, preached on the subject in 1862. In the sermon he pictured Africa as a land that would soon be developed as a great civilization, whose "peculiarity will be its moral element." He held that the "Gospel is to achieve some of its more beautiful triumphs in that land." Just as the "predictions" that God would enlarge Japheth have been fulfilled, since the "all-conquering descendants of Japheth have gone to every clime, and have planted themselves on almost every shore," so too would God's "blessed promise" to Ham be fulfilled.[53]

Abolitionists, intent on demolishing the Biblical proslavery arguments, acknowledged the centrality of Genesis 9 for their opponents. In 1838 Theodore Weld recognized that the prophecy of Noah was the major argument in the proslavery arsenal of biblical texts.[54] In _Uncle Tom's Cabin_, Harriet Beecher Stowe depicted the Northern versus Southern biblical debate in a rather contrived interchange among white passengers on a boat transporting slaves down the river. One parson declared, "It's undoubtedly the intention of Providence that the African race should be servants,--kept in a low condition.... 'Cursed be Canaan; a servant of servants shall he be,' the scripture says." Later, another minister countered by quoting the biblical text, "All things whatsoever ye would that men should do unto you, do ye even so unto them."[55] The Christian abolitionists did not fully understand why the Ham story captivated the Southern imagination. While they recognized its prominence in the proslavery arsenal of biblical texts, they never fully understood its symbolic persuasiveness.

The exponents of the story, on the other hand, were continually amazed that anyone would doubt that blacks were enslaved because of Noah's curse. Philip Schaff, a professor of church history at Mercersburg Theological Seminary in Pennsylvania, admitted that only Canaan was specifically mentioned in the curse but argued that this was due to "his close contact with the Israelites." Schaff claimed that "the curse ... has affected nearly the whole posterity of Ham.... [It] is simply a fact which no one can deny that the negro to this day is a servant of servants in our own midst."[56] One anonymous writer claimed that Ham was obviously cursed since "no person acquainted with ancient annals can deny that one race, the black, a branch of the Hametic stock, has, so far as is known, always been in a state of servitude."[57] J. C. Mitchell, a Presbyterian minister in Mobile, wrote that although the curse specifically mentioned Canaan, it "evidently includes Ham's descendants in the other branches" since "the descendants of Shem ... subdued the Canaanites ... and in later times we know that the descendants of Ham have been more or less the slaves of the descendants of Japheth."[58] For those who became persuaded by the story, it was true because the prophecy fit the facts and was being fulfilled in America. From a rational standpoint the argument is circular; the story did not, however, persuade because it was rational, but because it could easily be made to fit the attitudes and beliefs of those who supported slavery.

## Noah, the "Good Old Patriarch"

The Southern story-tellers also naturally embellished the story of Noah and his three sons by interpreting it in terms of the dominant political, social, and religious ideas of the Old South. The story then became symbolically persuasive because it reinforced prevalent attitudes about the nature of government and the planters' image both of themselves and of the ideal Southern plantation. Noah was not simply the father of Japheth, Shem, and Ham, but was the "vicegerent of heaven," in the words of Leander Ker, a military chaplain in the United States Army who was stationed at Fort Leavenworth.[59] According to another source "the patriarch Noah, being 600 years old, was now the head and father of the human family, the great representative of the race. He was the object of God's favor, and received from Him special and general directions for the government of the world."[60] Exponents of the story frequently tried to preserve Noah's moral character by suggesting that his inebriation was not a sin; he undoubtedly did not know the potency of the fermented grape since it had just been harvested for the first time. Noah was, according to the commentators, the "preacher of righteousness," "prophet of the Lord," "holy Noah," and especially "the good old patriarch."[61]

No one claimed that God had doomed an entire race

because Ham happened to see his father naked. While the story-tellers suggested a variety of wicked acts that might be involved, they all agreed that Ham had dishonored his father. John Bell Robinson, a Methodist minister in Pennsylvania, asked rhetorically whether God punished "Adam and the whole human family simply because he ate the fruit." No, the particular offence represented Adam's rebellion against God. If one, however, were to compare the mere acts, Robinson claimed that "Ham's was a thousand times more flagitious than Adam's. In Adam's case there was no harm in simply eating the apple...."[62] Ker explained that since Noah was "the vicegerent of heaven," Ham's "crime of disobeying, insulting and mocking" his parent was a "deliberate and willful offence" against "the moral government of God."[63] "The patriarchs," wrote an anonymous author, "were Rulers and Priests as well as Fathers." God himself instituted the family, which "is the most important, the happiest, and the most blessed institution with which he has endowed the human race." And the family, he concluded, "is truly the foundation of all other government."[64] Ham's real offence, then, was an attack against the authority of the family and thereby against God's chosen institution for governing the human race.

According to Southern political and religious theory, the goal of all governmental institutions was the preservation of society by means of controlling man's sinful nature. Southerners believed that the family was the most fundamental institution of social control, the best model for all other forms of government. C. Vann Woodward, drawing upon the work of Peter Laslett, writes that one of the striking differences between the Puritan settlement in Virginia and that in Massachusetts was the Southerners' emphasis on the family as the basic unit for organizing society. Virginians came predominantly from a region of England--middle-eastern Kent--where the philosophy of Sir Robert Filmer, the chief antagonist of John Locke, exalted the family as the foundation of government.[65]

Filmer's basic presupposition, according to Laslett, was that the Bible contained God's will for the proper structuring of society. Filmer argued that Adam set up a patriarchal form of government where authority resided in the father and passed to the eldest son after his father's death. Noah somewhat altered the unitary rule of one person over the entire earth by dividing up the world among his sons. The patriarchal family is not to be confused with the contemporary nuclear family, for apprentices and other servants became part of the personal, social dynamics of family life. The employer not only regulated the worker's production, to use modern terms, but also controlled his personal life as well. Peter Laslett summarizes the social order in England before industrialization by stressing that the "economic organization was domestic organization, and relationships were rigidly regulated by the social system, by the content of Christianity itself." A large household might contain 13 people, including children. The largest family that historians have found, excluding royal and clerical groups such as the king's court and Christian monasteries, contained 37 people, extremely small by industrial standards. The "gentlemen," or the heads of the larger households, rarely did manual labor, but engaged in scholarship, in community activities such as sitting on local courts, and in managing their estates.[66]

Filmer not only reflected the patriarchal society that he lived in, but also extolled its virtues and based his political theory on it. Many of the early settlers in Virginia were friends, relatives, and acquaintances of Filmer who espoused his ideas. For example, his brother Henry settled on the plantation of Laus Deo. Significantly, the great Virginia families of the eighteenth century were descended from Filmer--the Washingtons, the Berkeleys, the Randolphs, and the Byrds.[67] Judging from a letter of William Byrd II in 1726, Sir Robert not only contributed genes to the Virginia enterprise, but social attitudes as well:

> I have a large Family of my own, and my Doors are open to Every Body, yet I have no Bills to pay, and half-a-Crown will rest undisturbed in my Pocket for many Moons together. Like one of the Patriarchs, I have my Flocks and my Herds, my Bond-men and Bond-women, and every Soart of Trade amongst my own Servants, so that I live in a kind of Independence on everyone but Providence. However this Soart of Life is without expence, yet it is attended with a great deal of trouble. I must take care to keep all my people to their Duty, to set all the Springs in motion and make everyone draw his equal Share to carry the Machine forward.[68]

Southerners continued to champion the family as the ideal form of social control until at least the 1860's. The plantation economy undoubtedly reinforced the ideal of the patriarchal household in the South. The industrial revolution in England and the North necessarily separated economic organization from domestic and social relationships. But the South was primarily a rural society; even its major city, Charleston, depended on trade in the products of agriculture, and many large absentee rice planters lived there most of the year. Although industrialization was encouraged and indeed grew in the decade before the Civil War, the main sources of Southern wealth were the staple crops of cotton, tobacco, hemp, sugar, and rice. Most white families farmed a modest acreage with the help of few, if any, slaves. In 1860 fewer than 50,000 planters out of a population of eight million whites in the South owned as many as 20 slaves; fewer than 3000 had 100 or more; only 11 whites held over 500.[69]

Yet it was the bondage of blacks that particularly helped reinforce the patriarchal ideal among Southern whites. Abolitionists frequently attacked the ethics of slavery by pointing to the abuses and suffering of blacks in the South. For example, in Uncle Tom's Cabin, Harriet Beecher Stowe detailed accounts of young children torn from their parents, of slaves beaten severely at the whim of their masters, of marriages destroyed, and of women forced to become their masters' concubines. Judging from the angry response of Southerners, Stowe's attack touched a raw nerve. Almost without exception they expressed resentment that she had presented all slaveowners as morally corrupt tyrants. Interestingly, however, Stowe had never claimed that all slaveowners were tyrants, but only that the system of slavery was not able to check the brutality of those who were. (She even created Simon Legree, her most demonic character, as a recent emigrant from the North.) Conservative political leaders in the South, who insisted on checks against governmental abuse of power, understood that power tends to corrupt; even authority based on the natural distinctions among people could easily be misused. Thus, as Kenneth Greenberg has argued, Southerners who had never abused their own slaves were uneasy about the overly harsh masters in their midst.[70]

When the proponents of slavery incorporated the peculiar institution into the framework of the patriarchal family, they had their most emotionally satisfying defense. Thomas Cobb was one of many Southerners to paint an idyllic picture of patriarchal slavery:

> In short, the Southern slavery is a patriarchal,

> social system. The master is the head of his family. Next to wife and children, he cares for his slaves. He avenges their injuries, protects their persons, provides for their wants, and guides their labors. In return, he is revered and held as protector and master. Nine-tenths of the Southern masters would be defended by their slaves, at the peril of their own lives.[71]

Yet however emotionally satisfying it was for the plantation owners to picture themselves as the patriarchal successors of Noah and Abraham, Southerners never completely resolved the conflict between this idyllic image and the harsh economic realities of the plantation and the legal definition of slaves as chattel.[72]

Eugene Genovese has, nevertheless, documented that Southern planters were not merely posturing when they defined their relationships with their slaves paternalistically. They might believe that the slaves of other planters would run away or rebel, but they often expressed amazement in their diaries when one of their own "family" proved "disloyal"; they would lament the slave's "lack of gratitude" for past kindnesses and would write off the whole black race as a "selfish" lot.[73] Frederick Douglass substantiated the white planters' paternalistic attitudes when narrating an episode just after his first, aborted attempt to run away. His master's mother was sure that her Henry and John "never would have thought of running away" if Frederick had not put the idea into their heads. She angrily cursed the alleged instigator while exonerating her boys and giving them biscuits. Douglass explained that she "was much attached, after the southern fashion, to Henry and John, they having been reared from childhood in her house."[74] Gilbert, one of the ringleaders in Gabriel Prosser's planned insurrection, while agreeing that his master and mistress would have to be killed, also knew that "he could not do it himself ... because they raised him."[75]

Slaveowners unrealistically expected gratitude from blacks who had been part of "the family" for years and were disappointed when the ex-slaves could express their true attitudes after emancipation. It was not uncommon, however, for ex-slaves to express affectionate sentiments for their old masters. To a certain extent blacks accepted and therefore reinforced the white planters' patriarchal attitudes--but for very different reasons. The slave appealed to his master's self-image as a benevolent patriarch to lessen some of the worst burdens of slavery such as punishment by harsh overseers and brutalization by the patrollers who were usually little more than gangs of legalized ruffians. By appealing to their master as patriarch slaves might also gain special favors for the black community.[76]

If blacks tolerated and even encouraged paternalism for physical survival, the white planters maintained it for moral purposes. As long as planters could view themselves as presiding over a patriarchal family, they could also view the atrocities of slavery as rare. For did not the family balance self-interest and social responsibility? White Southerners argued that most fathers naturally love their children, and husbands cherish their wives. If natural affection failed, however, enlightened self-interest generally protected the weaker members of the family (women and children) from exploitation. The success of the family depended on the co-operation of all its members; if children were not well cared for, they would not be able to contribute to the economic prosperity of the parents, or if wives were abused, marital antagonism would destroy the trust necessary for building a common future.[77] Similarly, the proponents of slavery contended, the masters and mistresses regarded their blacks affectionately. Even when that was not true, the planters benefited economically when their slaves were satisfied, healthy, and well fed. Slaves, after all, represented a significant investment. Thus, since slavery operated within the patriarchal framework of the family, white Southerners believed that atrocities were rare.[78]

Of course, sinful people could occasionally abuse their God-given patriarchal authority. Whoever held control over another might misuse that power: husbands have tyrannized wives, school teachers and parents have abused children, judges have perverted justice by seeking personal gain. But the authority embodied in such institutions could not be eliminated or even structurally changed to eradicate or lessen inequality since the very basis of institutions was the exercise of hierarchical control by those best suited by nature to rule.[79]

Southerners argued that a master's control over his slaves was "precisely the kind of slavery to which every abolitionist in the country dooms his wife and children," in the words of the agricultural reformer, Solon Robinson.[80] If Northerners accepted the authority structure within the family, such Southerners as the social theorist, George Fitzhugh, could logically contend that the ethical justice of slavery for blacks hinged on the following question: "are the negroes, as a class, weak, helpless, improvident or dependent, like women and children, and therefore, as a class, to be subjected to slavery; or are they fitted generally for the offices and functions of masters?"[81]

The proponents of slavery contended that all civilizations forced certain classes of people to labor for the rest of society. Without coercion few people would voluntarily work at tasks of common drudgery and there could be no social progress. The moral question was, therefore, what type of social compulsion produced the maximum human progress without severe consequences for the individual? In some countries kings and other kinds of despots forced their subjects to work for the state; in ancient Egypt people were slaves of the pharaoh. In contemporary times a more impersonal monetary system replaced such overt control. People were forced to work or starve, and thus, necessity and want compelled the common laborer to slave for the capitalist and indirectly for the whole society.

The Southern critique of capitalism in the antebellum period rivalled that of the early European socialists, though of course from a very different point of view. Proponents of slavery believed it hypocrisy for abolitionists to attack the abuses of slavery while ignoring far worse crimes against humanity perpetrated under capitalism--such as the plight of the poor English laborers who were forced at an early age to work in mines and factories up to 16 hours a day without sufficient food and lodging. When the hirelings were no longer useful, they became discarded cripples left to starve. The peculiar institution in the South was, according to the proponents of slavery, a happy system in comparison to such an abusive system: children were rarely overworked on the plantation, the life expectancy of slaves was comparable to that of whites in the slave states, older slaves who could no longer work were adequately housed and fed as long as they lived. Robert M. T. Hunter of Virginia made the comparison poignantly in a speech before the United States Senate in 1850:

> Will any man pretend to say that the servitude of the laborer, in the crowded populations of Europe, is voluntary? Go into the English Colliery, and tell me if those boys who are hitched to carts by

> dog chains, to draw coals, through the dark, damp, and narrow passages of the pits, are voluntary servants.... In point of moral culture, and physical comfort, who can doubt that the Southern slave is the superior?[82]

George Fitzhugh, a Virginia lawyer and popular essayist, raised the defense of slavery and critique of capitalism to its most theoretical level. He anticipated Marx's "labor theory of value": "The profits, made from free labor, are the amount of the products of such labor, which the employer, by means of the command which capital or skill gives him, takes away, exacts, or 'exploitates' from the free laborer." Capitalism selfishly built on the principle that employers deserved "the lion's share" of the value created by the worker. Therefore, so-called "free laborers" were in reality "slaves" without the basic rights of food, housing, and protection that blacks enjoyed in the South. The worker was "a 'slave without a master,' and his oppressors, 'cannibals all.'"[83]

Fitzhugh acknowledged that the early European socialists and communists rightly dissected capitalism and analyzed its shortcomings. He admitted that his philosophy was influenced by such men as Saint Simon and Fourier. Yet his world view prevented him from adopting the socialist solution to capitalist society. Socialists, Fitzhugh believed, presumptously attempted to create a new social order. They were bound to fail because "social bodies ... are the works of God." The Christian world should turn to the Bible for guidance in understanding God's will. God had established social laws in order to check man's sinful, selfish nature; the basis for all divine social regulations was patriarchal: "Love and veneration for the family is with us not only a principle, but probably a prejudice and a weakness." Domestic slavery, like the institution of marriage, provided mutual advantages for both the controller and the controlled. It was in the master's interest to care for the slaves, and in the slave's interest to work for the well-being of the master's family: "A Southern farm is a sort of joint stock concern ... in which the master furnishes the capital and skill, and the slaves the labor, and divide the profits, not according to each one's input, but according to each one's wants and necessities."[84]

Although Fitzhugh thought that <u>all</u> blacks needed to be controlled by masters, his defense of slavery as a patriarchal institution did not rest primarily on racism. He even maintained that white slavery would be preferable to the situation of the free laborer whenever the antagonism between capital and labor became so great that workers' wages were inadequate.[85] While no other Southerner explicitly suggested that white slavery could be justified or should be established, others claimed that the Southern peculiar institution provided a humane form of compulsion.

Governor Hammond of South Carolina wrote that while capitalism might be more economical, it was certainly less humane: "We must, therefore, content ourselves with our dear labor, under the consoling reflection that what is lost to us, is gained to humanity; and that, inasmuch as our slave costs us more than your free man costs you, by so much is he better off." Unlike despotic systems where rulers far removed from human suffering governed their subjects by whim, or unlike capitalism where impersonal forces of supply and demand caused personal hardships, Southern slaves were part of the masters' own extended families. As part of the planters' capital, slaves were well fed and adequately sheltered, since the plantations' success depended on their health and strength.[86] In 1838 Calhoun remarked in the United States Senate that "Every plantation is a little community, with the master at its head, who concentrates in himself the united interests of capital and labor, of which he is the common representative."[87]

## NOTES

[1]Alexander Hamilton Stephens, "Speech ... Known as 'The Corner Stone Speech,'" Alexander H. Stephens in Public and Private, ed. Henry Cleveland (Philadelphia: National, 1866), p. 721.

[2]Edmund S. Morgan, American Slavery American Freedom (New York: W. W. Norton, 1975), pp. 118-23.

[3]Both Morgan, chs. 5 and 6, and Clement Eaton, A History of the Old South (New York: Macmillan, 1949), ch. 2, contain excellent discussions on the origin of the Southern plantations. See also Comer Vann Woodward, American Counterpoint (Boston: Little, Brown, 1971), pp. 16-21.

[4]See Winthrop D. Jordan, White over Black (1968; Baltimore: Penguin Books, 1969), ch. 2; Morgan, ch. 15; and Eaton, pp. 36-46. All three variously explain the

movement of the plantation economy from white indentured servitude to black slavery.

[5]Charles S. Sydnor, The Development of Southern Sectionalism 1819-1848, vol. V of A History of the South, ed. W. H. Stephenson and E. M. Coulter (Baton Rouge: Louisiana State University Press, 1948), pp. 6-8, 250; Clement Eaton, The Growth of Southern Civilization 1790-1860 (New York: Harper & Brothers, 1961), pp. 4-5; Eaton, History, pp. 231-34, 373; and Jordan, pp. 319-21.

[6]Joseph Clarke Robert, The Road from Monticello (1941; rpt. New York: AMS, 1970), passim.

[7]Sydnor, p. 95.

[8]Robert, passim; and Sydnor, pp. 6, 95, 227-28.

[9]Robert, pp. 45, 49-52.

[10]Hilrie Shelton Smith, In His Image but ... (Durham, N.C.: Duke University, 1972), pp. 70-72; and Sydnor, pp. 95-97.

[11]Sydnor, pp. 7-14; and Eaton, History, pp. 227-30.

[12]Eaton, Growth, pp. 49-53; Eaton, History, pp. 253-55; and Sydnor, p. 258. The rise of the price of slaves between 1800 and 1860 is more significant when one considers that the wholesale price index for "all commodities" declined from 129 to 93 in the same period (100 is for base years 1910-1914); see U.S. Bureau of the Census, The Statistical History of the United States from Colonial Times to the Present (Stamford, Conn.: Fairfield, 1965), pp. 115-16.

[13]See Morgan, ch. 15.

[14]Thomas Roderick Dew, "Professor Dew on Slavery," The Pro-Slavery Argument (1852; rpt. New York: Negro Universities Press, 1968), pp. 358, 422. See also Matthew Estes, A Defence of Negro Slavery (Montgomery: Press of the "Alabama Journal," 1846), pp. 142-58, 182-84; William Harper, "Harper on Slavery," Pro-Slavery Argument, pp. 35, 67-73; and Thornton Stringfellow, Scriptural and Statistical Views in Favor of Slavery (1841; 4th ed., Richmond: J. W. Randolph, 1856), p. 137.

[15]In 1800 Virginians learned that Gabriel Prosser had

organized a guerrilla force of about 200 slaves to terrorize Richmond and create the conditions for a more general uprising. In 1811 about 400 slaves marched into New Orleans in arms under the leadership of Charles Deslondes. In 1822 Carolinians discovered Denmark Vesey's and "Gullah Jack's" plot to attack Charleston. In 1831 Nat Turner led 70 blacks in terrorizing Southampton County, Va., killing nearly 60 men, women, and children.

On the rebelliousness of slaves, see Eugene D. Genovese, Roll Jordan Roll (1972; New York: Vintage Books, 1976), pp. 587-98, 613-37, 648-57; Jordan, pp. 391-402; Gerald W. Mullin, Flight and Rebellion (New York: Oxford University Press, 1972); Kenneth Stampp, The Peculiar Institution (1956; New York: Alfred A. Knopf, 1968), ch. 3; and John W. Blassingame, The Slave Community (New York: Oxford University Press, 1972), ch. 4 and passim.

[16]Sydnor, pp. 2-5.

[17]Dew, pp. 287, 328, 444.

[18]John Caldwell Calhoun, The Works, ed. Richard K. Crallé, 6 vols. (1851-56; New York: D. Appleton and Co., 1888), V, 204-5.

[19]George Fitzhugh, "The Black and White Races of Men," De Bow's Review 30 (April 1861), 451; William A. Smith, Lectures on the Philosophy and Practice of Slavery (Nashville: Stevenson & Evans, 1856), p. 73; John H. Van Evrie, Negroes and Negro "Slavery" (3rd ed., 1863; rpt. Miami: Mnemosyne, 1969), p. 111; and J. H. Guenebault, ed., Natural History of the Negro Race (Charleston: D. J. Dowling, 1837), p. vii. Chapter IV, below, will explore the racial views of white Southerners in more detail.

[20]Kenneth Greenberg, "Revolutionary Ideology and the Proslavery Argument," The Journal of Southern History 42 (Aug. 1976), 365-84.

[21]Calhoun, I, 1-4, 57-58; III, 180; IV, 507, 512.

[22]Calhoun, I, 1-6, 58. Clinton Rossiter has described the ideal conservative's belief: "If human nature in general can never be much improved, each individual may nevertheless bring his own savage and selfish impulses under control." Conservatism in America, 2nd ed. (1962; New York: Alfred A. Knopf, 1966), p. 25.

[23]Calhoun, I, 56; III, 179; IV, 509-11.

[24]Calhoun, I, 7-8.

[25]Harper, pp. 5-6; W. A. Smith, pp. 28, 116-20, 61-69; Stephens, p. 721; William Gilmore Simms, "The Morals of Slavery," Pro-Slavery Argument, pp. 250-251; James Henry Hammond, "Hammond's Letters on Slavery," Pro-Slavery Argument, pp. 109-10; Hammond, Remarks ... on the Question of Receiving Petitions for the Abolition of Slavery (Washington City [sic; D.C.]: Duff Green, 1836), p. 15; Thomas R. R. Cobb, An Inquiry into the Law of Negro Slavery in the United States of America (1858; rpt. New York: Negro Universities Press, 1968), p. clxix; Francis Wilkenson Pickens, Speech ... on the Abolition Question (Washington, D.C.: Gales & Seaton, 1836).

[26]Rossiter writes that political conservatives in America have always been strongly influenced by religion, and in turn have supported established, orthodox churches: "The mortar that holds together the mosaic of Conservatism is religious feeling." Most American conservatives, Rossiter observes, have been Christians and therefore "prefer to call the motivation for iniquitous and irrational behavior by its proper name: Original Sin." The "great truth" of conservatism that "men are grossly unequal" rests squarely on the doctrine of human depravity (pp. 22-24, 42).

[27]W. A. Smith, p. 104; John Fletcher, Studies on Slavery (Natchez, Miss.: Jackson Warner, 1852), p. 246; John Leadley Dagg, The Elements of Moral Science (1859; New York: Sheldon & Company, 1860), p. 353; and Nathan Lord, A Northern Presbyter's Second Letter (Boston: Little, Brown, 1855), pp. 41-42.

[28]W. A. Smith, pp. 105-7, 129, and passim.

[29]Dagg, pp. 371-72.

[30]Cobb, p. 63.

[31]James A. Sloan, The Great Question Answered (Memphis: Hutton, Gallaway & Co., 1857), p. 73; and Calhoun, IV, 508. See also Thornton Stringfellow, Slavery (1841; 4th ed., Richmond: J. W. Randolph, 1856), pp. 4-5; W. A. Smith, pp. 65-66; George Fitzhugh, "The Counter Current,

or Slavery Principle," De Bow's Review 21 (July 1856), 95; and George Fitzhugh, "The Black and White Races," p. 454.

[32]Elizabeth Janeway has explored the mythic significance of the biblical creation account in relation to stereotypes about the inferiority of women in Man's World, Woman's Place: A Study in Social Mythology (New York: William Morrow and Company, 1971). Her first-rate study helped me understand not only the Eve story's mythic significance, but also the general importance of mythic thought in Western culture.

On the issue of biblical thinking as the basis for social and political theory, see Gordon J. Schochet, Patriarchalism in Political Thought (New York: Basic Books, 1975).

[33]Sloan, pp. 68-75; see also Lord, pp. 41-42; Fletcher, pp. 433-36; [Frederick Dalcho], Practical Considerations Founded on the Scriptures (Charleston: A. E. Miller, 1823), p. 8; Robert Lewis Dabney, A Defense of Virginia (1867; rpt. New York: Negro Universities Press, 1969), p. 102; and Josiah Priest, Slavery (Albany, N.Y.: C. Van Benthuysen, 1843), pp. 82-83.

[34]Dagg, p. 344.

[35]John England, "Letters to the Hon. John Forsyth, on the Subject of Domestic Slavery," The Works, ed. Ignatius A. Reynolds, 5 vols. (Baltimore: John Murphy, 1849), III, 119, 191. See also H. O. R., The Governing Race (Washington, D.C.: Thomas McGill, 1860), pp. 4-7.

[36]Sloan, p. 61 (emphasis added).

[37]Priest's works were popular. His Slavery was reprinted five times in eight years. His two other most widely read works were American Antiquities and Discoveries in the West (Albany, N.Y.: Hoffman & White, 1833), five printings, and Stories of the Revolution (Albany, N.Y.: Hoffman & White, 1836), four printings. Other writings included A View of the Expected Christian Millennium (Albany, N.Y.: Loomis, 1827); The Wonders of Nature and Providence Displayed (Albany, N.Y.: J. Priest, 1825); Stories of Early Settlers in the Wilderness (Albany, N.Y.: J. Munsell, 1837); and several captivity narratives.

[38]Priest, Slavery, pp. 15, 27-28. Subsequent citations of "Priest" in this chapter refer to Slavery.

[39]Priest, pp. 15-20, 27-36; Dalcho, p. 11; Sloan, pp. 55, 58-62, 78-80; Fletcher, pp. 440-42, 464-77, 483-502; Estes, pp. 49-50; Samuel Davies Baldwin, Dominion; or, The Unity and Trinity of the Human Race (Nashville: E. Stevenson and F. A. Owen, 1857), p. 232; and Leander Ker, Slavery Consistent with Christianity (Weston, Mo.: Finch & O'Gormon, Reporter Office, 1853), pp. 9-11.

[40]Thomas Newton, Dissertations on the Prophecies, 2nd ed., 3 vols. (London: J. and R. Tonson, 1759), I, 15, 19-24. Philip Schaff cites Bishop Newton and paraphrases his complete argument in Slavery and the Bible (Chambersburg, Pa.: M. Kieffer & Co., 1861), pp. 4-7; Sloan also cites Newton, p. 83.

[41]Augustin Calmet, Calmet's Dictionary of the Holy Bible, ed., Charles Taylor (London: W. Stratford, Crown-Court, Temple-Bar, 1800). See also Calmet, Fragments, ed. Charles Taylor (London: W. Stratford, Crown-Court, Temple-Bar, 1801), p. 37. At least one American author cited Calmet directly, African Servitude (New York: Davies & Kent, 1860), p. 16.

[42]The quotation is from Louis Ginzberg, The Legends of the Jews, 7 vols. (Philadelphia: Jewish Publication Society of America, 1909-1938), I, 168-69. See also I, 166, 170-73, 175, 177, 326-27; II, 15, 117, 288-89, 324; III, 267, 452; V, 55-56, 182, 188, 191-92, 200, 265; VI, 4, 117. Ginzberg's work includes extensive documentation of the Jewish midrashim about the story of Noah and Ham.

[43]Samuel Sewall, "The Selling of Joseph: A Memorial," Racial Thought in America, Vol. I, From the Puritans to Abraham Lincoln: A Documentary History, ed. Louis Ruchames (New York: Universal Library, Grosset & Dunlap, 1970), pp. 49-50.

[44]John Woolman, "Some Considerations on the Keeping of Negroes," Journal and Essays of John Woolman, ed. Amelia M. Gummere (1774; New York: Macmillan, 1922), p. 355.

[45]Quoted in David Christy, "Cotton Is King: or Slavery in the Light of Political Economy," Cotton Is King, and Pro-Slavery Arguments, ed. E. N. Elliott (Augusta, Ga.: Pritchard, Abbott & Loomis, 1860), p. 163.

[46]Quoted in Christy, p. 165.

[47][Edwin Clifford Holland], A Refutation of the Calumnies Circulated against the Southern and Western States (Charleston: A. E. Miller, 1822), p. 41.

[48]Stephens, pp. 722-23. See also Sen. Robert Toombs, "Slavery: Its Constitutional Status, and Its Influence on Society and the Colored Race," De Bow's Review 20 (May 1856), 581-82; and Cobb, p. 17.

[49]Cobb, pp. xxxv-xxxvi.

[50]Mark Twain, Pudd'nhead Wilson (1894; New York: Grove Press, 1955), ch. X, pp. 101-2.

[51]James W. C. Pennington, A Text Book of the Origin and History, &c. &c. of the Colored People (Hartford, Conn.: L. Skinner, 1841), pp. 9-13.

[52]Gayraud S. Wilmore, Black Religion and Black Radicalism (New York: Doubleday, 1972), pp. 164-68.

[53]Edward W. Blyden, "The Call of Providence to the Descendants of Africa in America," Negro Social and Political Thought 1850-1920: Representative Texts, ed. Howard Brotz (New York: Basic Books, 1966), p. 121.

[54][Theodore Dwight Weld], The Bible against Slavery 3rd ed. (New York: American Anti-Slavery Society, 1838), p. 46. See Chapter I, p. 5, above.

[55]Harriet Beecher Stowe, Uncle Tom's Cabin (1852; New York: Harper and Row, 1965), pp. 125-26.

[56]Schaff, p. 6.

[57]H. O. R., pp. 8-9.

[58]J. C. Mitchell, A Bible Defence of Slavery and the Unity of Mankind (Mobile, Ala.: J. Y. Thompson, 1861), p. 5.

[59]Ker, p. 10.

[60]African Servitude, p. 5.

[61]Schaff, p. 5; Mitchell, p. 4; John J. Flournoy, An Essay in the Origin, Habits, &c. of the African Race (New

York: n.p., 1835), p. 4; and John Bell Robinson, Pictures of Slavery and Anti-Slavery (1863; rpt. Miami: Mnemosyne, 1969), p. 20.

[62]Robinson, pp. 53-55, 20, 26.

[63]Ker, p. 10.

[64]African Servitude, pp. 4-5.

[65]Woodward, pp. 135-36; and Robert Filmer, Patriarcha and Other Political Works of Sir Robert Filmer, ed. and intro. Peter Laslett (Oxford: Basil Blackwell, 1949), pp. 8-10. See also Rossiter, pp. 28-32, showing that American conservatives have generally believed in the intrisicality of the family as the foundation of government.

[66]Filmer, pp. 12-15, 25, 58-59; Peter Laslett, The World We Have Lost, 2nd ed. (New York: Charles Scribner's Sons, 1973), ch. 1 and passim; the quotation is on p. 4.

[67]See Laslett's Introduction, pp. 2-10, in Filmer.

[68]Quoted in Mullin, p. vii.

[69]Clement Eaton, Growth, pp. 1, 8-10; Sydnor, pp. 3-4; Avery O. Craven, The Growth of Southern Nationalism 1848-1861, vol. VI of A History of the South, ed. W. H. Stephenson & E. M. Coulter (Baton Rouge: Louisiana State University Press, 1953), pp. 7-13.

[70]Stowe, passim; Greenberg, pp. 373-75.

[71]Cobb, p. ccxviii. See also W. A. Smith, pp. 11-12, 39, 47; Lord, passim; Pickens, p. 12; and [Patrick H. Mell], Slavery (Penfield Ga.: Benj. Brantley, 1844), passim.

[72]Genovese, pp. 25-49.

[73]Genovese, pp. 70-75, 133-49.

[74]Frederick Douglass, Life and Times of Frederick Douglass (1892; New York: Bonanza Books, 1962), pp. 169-70.

[75]Quoted in Mullin, p. 147.

[76]Genovese, pp. 133-49.

[77]Garnett, "The South and the Union," De Bow's Review 19 (July 1855), 42-43; Lord, p. 45; and George Fitzhugh, Slavery Justified (Fredericksburg, Va.: Recorder Printing Office, 1850), p. 14.

[78]See Calhoun, III, 180; Cobb, p. ccxviii; Fletcher, p. 23; Pickens, p. 15; Lord, p. 20; Garnett, pp. 42-43; and Solon Robinson, "Negro Slavery at the South," De Bow's Review 7 (Sept. 1849), 216, 220.

[79]Lord, p. 23; Mell, p. 19; Fletcher, pp. 25, 203, 206-7; Simms, p. 127.

[80]Solon Robinson, p. 216.

[81]George Fitzhugh, "The Counter Current," p. 95. See also Fletcher, pp. 25, 203; George S. Sawyer, Southern Institutes (1859; rpt. Miami: Mnemosyne, 1969), p. 236; and Frederick Augustus Ross, Slavery Ordained of God (1857; rpt. Miami: Mnemosyne, 1969), p. 53.

[82]Robert Mercer Taliaferro Hunter, "Mr. Hunter on the English Negro Apprentice Trade," De Bow's Review 24 (June 1858), 496. See also William J. Grayson, "The Hireling and the Slave," De Bow's Review 21 (Sept. 1856), 249-51; Solon Robinson, pp. 222-23; Cobb, p. xxvi; Hammond, "Letters," p. 139; Harper, pp. 19, 24-27; Sawyer, pp. 246-86; and W. A. Smith, p. 150.

[83]George Fitzhugh, Cannibals All!, ed. Comer Vann Woodward (1857; Cambridge, Mass.: Belknap Press of Harvard University, 1960), pp. 13, 15, 31, 69, 87.

[84]Fitzhugh, Cannibals, pp. 22, 26, 192; Fitzhugh, "Southern Thought Again," De Bow's Review 23 (Nov. 1857), 452-53; and George Fitzhugh, Sociology for the South (1854; rpt. New York: Burt Franklin, 1965), p. 48.

[85]George Fitzhugh, "Southern Thought," De Bow's Review 23 (Oct. 1857), 339, 348.

[86]Hammond, "Letters," pp. 121-22. See also Fletcher, pp. 113, 219; Sawyer, pp. 227-30; Cobb, p. ccxiii; Garnett, pp. 45-47; and Fitzhugh, Cannibals, p. 18.

## Chapter IV

# THE SIN OF HAM AND WHITE RACISM

In the 1830's white Southerners increasingly came to justify slavery by claiming it was necessary to control an inherently inferior race. Thus racial prejudice became explicitly joined with the defense of slavery in a full-blown racism. In speeches before the United States Senate in 1836 and 1837, John C. Calhoun declared that slavery was "a positive good," because it controlled an inferior people "of different origin, and distinguished by color, and other physical differences, as well as intellectual." As long as whites and blacks lived in the same land, blacks would have to be enslaved. Emancipation would not overcome the blacks' inferiority, according to Calhoun, because "the causes lie too deep in the principles of our nature to be surmounted."[1] By the 1840's the American School of Ethnology made belief in the innate inferiority of the black race scientifically respectable. Although Southerners generally repudiated the polygenetic theory that blacks originated as a separate species, they nevertheless accepted the investigators' conclusions that the black race was vastly inferior to whites. The racists' picture of blacks as physically ugly, mentally retarded, and morally delinquent did not easily conform to the planter's self-image as a patriarch governing a fairly contented family. How did the Southern proponents of slavery join racist beliefs with patriarchal attitudes? How did the story of Noah and his three sons explain the origin of racial differences without compromising the ideal of the patriarchal family?

## White Racism

The word "racist" has been used in so many contexts that it has become a very imprecise term. Here "racist" refers to the belief that the black race was inherently inferior to the white. While racism and the advocacy of slavery were intertwined in America, not all racists supported slavery and not all abolitionists were free from racism. For example, Hinton Rowan Helper, a North Carolina shopkeeper and California gold prospector, published an abolitionist book in 1857 that was very influential in the North. The Impending Crisis of the South championed the cause of the poor white worker who was unable to compete with slave labor. Helper amassed statistics to show that slavery had retarded the growth of the South and had prevented the region from sharing in the wealth of the nation. The book was important in the campaign of 1860 when the Republican Party broadened its appeal to farmers and working-class whites. Other antislavery leaders tried to use the book, written by a native Southerner and son of a yeoman farmer, as a wedge to drive apart the interests of the poor Southern whites and the rich planters. George M. Fredrickson believes that The Impending Crisis probably even surpassed Uncle Tom's Cabin in feeding "the fires of sectional controversy leading up to the Civil War." Yet Helper, one of the most virulent racists in the country, wanted blacks to be liberated only to be exported or exterminated. Although Helper muted his racism in The Impending Crisis to gain a wider appeal among his Northern antislavery allies, two books he published after the Civil War were among the most racist ever issued in America.[2]

The debate before the Virginia legislature on the question of abolishing slavery also shows the danger of equating antislavery sentiment with belief in the equality of the two races. While a few antislavery legislators argued that slavery was antithetical to the Declaration of Independence and the rights of man, most of them discussed the political and economic welfare of whites. The peculiar institution, they contended, burdened the Southern economy and even caused the current recession in Virginia. The proslavery delegates mainly discussed the slaveowners' property rights, asserting that slaves should not be emancipated without compensation and that reimbursing the planters would bankrupt the state. They thought the colonization schemes before the legislature wildly impractical. No one suggested that slaves might be emancipated without simultaneous deportation. Even the Quaker petition asked that resettlement territory be acquired outside Virginia. Antislavery and proslavery legislators agreed that racial differences precluded emancipated blacks from living peacefully in the same nation with whites.[3]

There is little historical evidence about the legal and social standing of the blacks in the first two decades after they arrived in Virginia in 1619. After 1640 blacks were increasingly held in perpetual bondage, and by 1660 slavery was established by statute. The paucity of hard data has left room for chicken-and-egg arguments among historians on the relationship between racial prejudice and slavery. Some maintain that blacks were enslaved because of white bias, others that enslavement caused white prejudice. According to Jordan the two occurred simultaneously: "Rather than slavery causing 'prejudice,' or vice versa, they seem rather to have generated each other. Both were, after all, twin aspects of a general debasement of the Negro."[4]

The accounts of the first Englishmen who explored the African Continent contained racial prejudice, and early Americans generally treated blacks as inferiors, according to evidence adduced by Jordan. Writings abound in America before 1800 disparaging the blacks' physical features, their unrefined civilization, and their depraved morals, particularly sexual licentiousness. Yet, while the founding fathers were proclaiming that all men were created equal, few, if any, writers on race suggested that black inferiority was innate. Rather, theorists hypothesized that the blacks' mental and spiritual deficiencies would be corrected under the tutelage of white Christians. Samuel Stanhope Smith, a prominent Presbyterian clergyman, even suggested that the temperate climate in America might eventually ameliorate the blacks' unsightly appearance.[5]

Ironically, the author of the Declaration of Independence advanced "as a suspicion only, that the blacks, whether originally a distinct race, or made distinct by time and circumstances, are inferior to the whites in the endowments both of body and mind." Jefferson's observations led him to believe that while blacks were equal to whites in memory, they were probably inferior in reason, and were "dull, tasteless, and anomalous" in imagination. While he suggested that "nature has been less bountiful to them in the endowments of the head," he affirmed that the blacks' tendency toward immorality and crime was caused by environmental factors. As an example, he claimed that their "disposition to theft ... must be ascribed to their situation," since they owned no property and therefore did not benefit from laws that made private property secure. According to Jordan, these provisional suspicions of Jefferson "stood as the strongest suggestion of inferiority expressed by any native American" until well into the nineteenth century when Southerners began to ground their aesthetic feelings, judgmental attitudes, and social mores in a thoroughgoing racist ideology.[6]

By the beginning of the nineteenth century Northern and Southern writers generally held that the physical distinctions between blacks and whites were permanent and understood that a change in climate would not eventually "whiten" the black race.[7] However, the antislavery faction, particularly in the North, continued to champion environmental explanations for the blacks' supposed mental and moral inferiority. Abolitionists believed that white prejudice and discrimination denied the emancipated Negro of rights and opportunities accorded to whites. Poverty and segregation promoted high rates of crime and ignorance among free blacks, and slavery encouraged immorality on plantations. Garrison and Weld, hoping to raise individual blacks above their group's fate, urged them to undercut doctrines stressing their innate moral and intellectual inferiority by demonstrating to the contrary.[8] Frederick Douglass told abolitionists in England that

> the greatest hindrance to the adoption of abolition principles by the people of the United States was the low estimate everywhere in that country placed upon the Negro as a man--that because of his assumed natural inferiority people reconciled themselves to his enslavement and oppression as being inevitable, if not desirable. The grand thing to be done, therefore, was to change this estimation by disproving his inferiority and demonstrating his capacity for a more exalted civilization than slavery and prejudice had assigned him.[9]

Only after the debate before the Virginia legislature did Southern writers begin to claim that blacks were inferior by nature, thus entwining the defense of slavery with a full-blown racism. Thomas R. Dew moved toward this position in his celebrated *Review of the Debate of the Virginia Legislature of 1831 and 1832*. In the opening paragraph Dew asserted that blacks were "vastly inferior" to whites "in the scale of civilization." He argued that emancipation in Santo Domingo had led to "the bloodiest and most shocking insurrection ever recorded in the annals of history"; that free blacks were the "drones and pests" of American society, since they were idle and prone to crime; that Africa was a barbarous land where superstition, cruelty, and murders showed the true character of the Negro. Slavery was the only possible antidote for the blacks' constitution: "There is nothing but slavery which can destroy those habits of indolence and sloth, and eradicate the character of improvidence and carelessness, which mark the independent savage." Yet Dew seemed uncertain whether the mental and moral inferiority was innate or environmentally conditioned. In some passages he heralded the dominant racial theory in the South after 1835 that black inferiority had an "inherent and intrinsic cause ... which will produce its effect under all circumstances." In other passages he agreed with the Virginia colonizationists, suggesting that "habits," or "customs," or "prejudices" had degraded the Negro.[10]

In the late 1830's a few Southern writers, bowing to logical consistency, did not altogether close the door on environmental theories. When they stressed the moral and intellectual progress that the black race had made in America under slavery, these Southerners wondered whether blacks might not someday equal whites. William Gilmore Simms, for example, wrote in 1837 that "it is possible that a time will come, when, taught by our schools, and made strong by our training, the negroes of the Southern States may arrive at freedom." Like most antebellum Southern writers, Simms justified slavery by pointing to the blacks' degraded morals and base intellect. For all practical purposes, however, the time was "very ... remote" when the black race might equal the white.[11] But most Southern writers on race after 1835 denounced the environmental hypothesis entirely, claiming that blacks were innately inferior to whites. They unhesitatingly declared that blacks were degraded "by nature" and therefore could never equal whites in morals or intelligence. By the early 1840's ethnologists began to validate the racists' views "scientifically."

While Southerners generally rejected that theory of the "American School of Ethnology" that blacks were created as a separate species, they did not necessarily spurn the ethnological evidence that pointed to the inherent inferiority of blacks. William Stanton has argued that "the American School was spared the reproach before history of having effectually furthered the cause of slavery," because Southerners largely rejected polygenesis in their devotion to the Bible. His analysis, however, too easily assumes that if Southerners repudiated the ethnologists' theory they must have also disavowed their conclusions about the inherent inferiority of the black race. On the contrary, nothing legitimized the "suspicions" of Thomas Jefferson more clearly than these scientific investigators. Christians who supported slavery took the defensive and began to incorporate unabashed racism into their world view.[12]

Popularizers of the new ethnology rarely attacked the biblical account of creation, and yet championed the proslavery argument using scientific terminology and documentation. Van Evrie, for example, insisted that there were several distinct "species" of mankind and derided those who believed that blacks and whites were "permanent varieties" since it was a "foolish dogma" to suppose that Negroes had "the same nature" as Caucasians. He maintained, however, that his arguments for black inferiority were equally valid, whether blacks were originally created as a separate species or "the Creator subsequently changed them into their present form."[13] The scientific racists who either ignored or rejected the biblical account of creation were able to argue more persuasively that blacks, being a separate species, could be enslaved without violating the principle of universal liberty for the Caucasian. Josiah Nott, a prominent spokesman for the scientific racists, wrote that "no one respects the rights of man more than ourselves ... or loves that beautiful abstraction, liberty, more than we do."[14]

Christian racists who accepted the Bible as the literal word of God had to maintain a difficult middle position. On the one hand, they believed that the African was a descendant of Adam and ought to be converted to Christianity, thus implying that a common brotherhood existed among men. On the other hand, they believed that the Negro was greatly inferior to the Caucasian and should be subordinate, thereby undercutting the notion of common descent. In the words of Wilson Carey McWilliams, "racism makes bad monotheism."[15]

## Noah's Curse and the Indelible Mark

The story of Ham helped mediate the central paradox of Christian brotherhood and enslavement by positing that God remolded the human race into three distinct races in the family of Noah. Thus the story of Ham could account for the blacks' supposed inferiority that the scientific racists were emphasizing. It could also explain the black color of Ham's descendants.

Interestingly, Englishmen had originally used the Genesis account to explain the origin of the Africans' blackness. According to evidence presented by Jordan, Caucasians had been prejudiced against the Negro's "blackness" when Englishmen first encountered the African. Jordan argues that whites in Elizabethan England had idealized beauty, particularly feminine beauty, as "white." White and black had symbolized pure and impure, good and evil, clean and dirty.[16] In eighteenth-century America, Jefferson expressed a similar aesthetic preference for "the fine mixtures of red and white" found in the Caucasian "to that eternal monotony ... that immovable veil of black which covers the emotions of the other race." He held that the "first difference," preventing the two races from living together on terms of equality, "is that of color."[17]

Thus aesthetic feelings about the "blackness" of the African race antedated the thoroughgoing racism in the antebellum South. John Woolman, an effective antislavery exponent among the Quakers in the eighteenth century, lamented that whites, who would never consider enslaving people of their own race, were willing to enslave Africans because of prejudice against their color. He argued that slavery based on color prejudice resulted from ignorance and lack of justice.[18] However, David Rice, a Presbyterian minister and a leading Kentucky abolitionist, admitted that he was not free of racial "pride," even though his "judgment" and "conscience" informed him that the "evil" of intermarriage between blacks and whites was culturally conditioned. While Rice admitted his aesthetic feelings against miscegenation, he believed that one day color prejudice would disappear since it was only a matter of education and social acceptance.[19]

White antebellum Southerners not only shared this repugnance to the blacks' color, but also increasingly viewed "blackness" as a symbol of the Africans' general inferiority. According to Dew, blackness was "a mark which no time can erase ... [and] the indelible symbol of his inferior condition."[20] Racists frequently argued that God had used color to indicate the rankings in the human family so that social and economic institutions would conform to his divine will. John H. Van Evrie, a New York physician, expressed this view succinctly in a book that was widely disseminated and enthusiastically accepted in the South:

> The Caucasian is white, the Negro is black; the first is the most superior, the latter the most inferior--and between these extremes of humanity are the intermediate races, approximating to the former or approaching the latter, just as the Almighty, in His boundless wisdom and ineffable beneficence, has seen fit to order it.[21]

In the 1840's and 50's the Southern proponents of

slavery increasingly wrote that physiological differences between the black and white races, epitomized by color variations, not only proved the Africans' innate inferiority, but also their unique suitability for enslavement. The racists supported their claims by turning to both the biblical story in Genesis 9 and to science. Scientific language frequently buttressed the story of Noah and his three sons. Although rational discourse can undermine the persuasiveness of such religious formulations, Southern arguments from anatomy, physiology, philology, ethnology, and history tended to substantiate the story of Ham by deflecting logical considerations from the story's core. In a word, Southerners used scientific language to block rather than to encourage further enquiry. Often the scientific language used by racists sounded impressive, but in reality was based on little, if any, evidence, and lacked the objective, dispassionate study necessary for a scientific understanding of the universe.

For example, Samuel A. Cartwright, an influential physician who practiced medicine in Alabama, Mississippi, and Louisiana, purportedly studied the physiological differences of blacks, contending that the blacks' constitution comprised "defective hematosis or atmospherization of the blood, conjoined with a deficiency of cerebral matter in the cranium, and an excess of nervous matter distributed to the organs of sensation and assimilation." These supposed physiological differences were "the true cause of that debasement of the mind which has rendered the people of Africa unable to take care of themselves," and the basis for "their indolence and apathy," and their preference for "idleness, misery and barbarism ... [to] industry and frugality."[22] Cartwright maintained that blacks, unlike whites, were governed by physiological laws that allowed them to work in the hot sun without hats (the black skin and a "cutilagenous membrane" that protected their eyes). Since the Negroes' strength and imitative ability were combined with a feeble will, they could easily be enslaved by physically weaker yet stronger-willed whites.[23]

To clinch the argument, Cartwright called Genesis "one of the most authentic books of the Bible," to show that his observations coincided with the "Divine Decree" that subordinated Ham to Japheth. It is remarkable, he wrote, that

> When the original Hebrew of the Bible is interrogated, we find, in the significant meaning of the original name of the negro, the identical fact set

> forth, which the knife of the anatomist at the dissecting-table has made appear; as if the revelations of anatomy, physiology and history, were a mere re-writing of what Moses wrote.

The very word Canaan, which Cartwright translated "submissive knee-bender," symbolized everything known about the nature of the black race from scientific study.[24]

George Fitzhugh wrote on the eve of the Civil War that physical laws are only rules originated by the Creator: "In Scriptural language, physical laws are called ordinances of heaven."[25] Sloan carried the philological argumentation further than Cartwright. After establishing that Ham meant "black," or "the mark of inferiority which God put upon the progenitor," he examined the meanings of the names of Ham's children and found that Cush denoted "black," Mizraim meant "restrained," Phut signified "despised," and Canaan conveyed "bowed down." Thus, he argued that "God, by His decree, and in consequence of his sin, has degraded Ham's posterity. The sentence, 'a servant of servants shall he be to his brethren,' has been fully exemplified in the past history of the three divisions of the human family."[26] Thus, in the words of Cartwright, "anatomy, physiology, history and theology ... sustain one another." And all the results of these disciplines could be authenticated by the divine ordinance in Genesis 9.[27]

The exponents of the Ham story all believed that Ham's progeny was black and they all agreed that blackness somehow epitomized the inferiority of the race. In the words of Sloan, "Ham's posterity are either black or dark colored, and thus bear upon their countenance the mark of inferiority which God put upon the progenitor."[28] Clearly, according to a couple of story-tellers, God changed the blacks' color as a sign that the whole race was doomed to involuntary servitude. Iveson L. Brookes, a South Carolina clergyman, insisted that Ham merited "decapitation" for his rebellion against God's authority, but that God, in his "wonderous mercy," punished him instead "by flattening his head, kinking his hair, and blackening his skin."[29] An anonymous writer claimed that "God has put his indelible mark" on the black race as "prima facie evidence" that they are indeed the descendants of Ham. Quoting Calmet's dictionary, the author wrote that when Noah cursed Ham, his "skin became black"; Noah, "seeing so surprising a change, was deeply affected."[30]

While this explanation of the origin of the blacks' color neatly dovetailed with racist attitudes about the blacks' appearance, the interpretation presented difficulties for those story-tellers who emphasized that God reconstituted humanity into three separate, color-coded races. Granted that God turned Ham black because he had sinned, why should he differentiate Japheth from Shem? Then, too, since the etymology of the word ham provided the principle proof that Ham was black, he must have been black when he entered the ark. No doubt for these reasons Josiah Priest insisted that God "superintended the formation of two of the sons of Noah in the womb of their mother." God only had to intervene supernaturally to produce the white and black races because Noah, like Adam, was created red.[31] Leander Ker, who believed that he was the first to give a public defense of slavery based on the Bible, claimed that God had reorganized the human family into three races so that they could adapt themselves more easily to the new climatic conditions on earth after the flood. Ham's complexion suited him for labor in the tropical regions.[32]

Even though Ker's and Priest's accounts of the origin of color are not directly grounded in racism, both authors included racial prejudice in their stories. Ker assumed that Noah gave Ham his name because of his dark complexion: "We may easily conceive that Noah would exclaim Ham! on seeing his son for the first time.--And it could not be expected that Noah would regard this child with the same paternal tenderness with which he regarded the others." Ker even suggested that resentment might partially "explain, if not palliate, the conduct of Ham in exposing his father's shame." Ker, like so many typical racists, assumed that standards of beauty were absolute, rather than environmentally conditioned.[33] Priest contended that both Ham's color and his name were "prophetic of Ham's character and fortunes" in his later life.[34] Blackness, therefore, still remained symbolic of God's curse against Ham's descendants for those authors who did not connect the coloring directly to Ham's sin and his subsequent punishment.

## Ham's Sin and the Character of His Descendants

The Southern story-tellers did, however, directly connect Ham's sin with their racist stereotypes. The nature of Ham's specific act came to symbolize the true nature of the blacks' mental inferiority coupled with their animal-like sensuality. Both the racists who sought guidance from the Bible and those who considered Types of Mankind as authoritative believed that blacks were mentally inferior to whites. Jefferson's "suspicion" that blacks were innately inferior to whites in their reasoning powers became accepted dogma in the antebellum South. But Christian racists, while carefully stating for the record that the blacks' intelligence could never equal that of the whites, still insisted that blacks possessed an intellectual nature that distinguished them from brutes. John Bachman, a Lutheran pastor in Charleston, insisted that the black man's "inferiority ... in intellect ... does not prove that he is not a man."[35] Thomas Smyth, a Presbyterian minister in Charleston, wrote that "in contrast to the lower animals," blacks are "capable of instruction, improvement, and useful skills."[36] Patrick Mell, a Baptist clergyman and educator in Georgia, believing in minimal education for slaves, lamented that the "officious interference of fanatics who are without our borders" forced Southerners to abandon instructional projects for slaves.[37] Most Christian racists, however, agreed with their scientific counterparts that the African could make little intellectual progress.

In order to show that this mental inferiority was not due to chance, racists turned to anatomy and physiology. George Morton, founder of the American School of Ethnology, had collected over a thousand skulls of persons belonging to many races. Although the internal capacity of the skull samples varied greatly among members of the same race, on the average Negro skull size was slightly smaller than Caucasian. Morton never claimed that brain size proved that blacks were less intelligent than whites, but his followers certainly did. Modern science has since discredited the correlation of brain size with intelligence, and the findings themselves were suspect since the skulls were never evaluated according to sex. The racist ethnographers who drew upon Morton's work overlooked the variations within each racial group. For example, in Morton's collection the largest skull of the "native African Family" had a greater capacity than the largest "Anglo-American" skull. Despite such contradictory evidence, physicians like Samuel Cartwright, Matthew Estes, Josiah Nott, and J. H. Van Evrie, popularizing Morton's work, declared that the "mean" size of the Negro skulls substantiated the belief in the innate mental inferiority of the whole black race.[38]

Southerners in the antebellum period who wrote on racial differences between whites and blacks continually supposed that blacks were "imitative" rather than "inventive" and "sensuous" rather than "intellectual." Popularizers of the ethnological research believed that their evidence supported these common opinions. They claimed that the greater facial angle of the Negro race showed that blacks had smaller cerebrums than whites. Some even held, without any supportive evidence, that blacks had larger cerebellums. The popularizers of science hypothesized that the cerebellum was the seat of sensations and bodily coordination. (According to modern science, this hypothesis is only partly accurate and greatly over-simplified.) "Science" therefore validated the long-standing prejudice that the black "is imitative, sometimes eminently so, but his mind is never inventive or suggestive," in the words of Judge Thomas R. R. Cobb of Georgia.[39] Cartwright also drew on science to support his belief that blacks were more coordinated and sensuous than whites. He held that the nature of the Negro's mind allowed him to "agitate every part of the body at the same time": "From the diffusion of the brain, as it were, into the various organs of the body, in the shape of nerves to minister to the senses, everything, from the necessity of such a conformation, partakes of sensuality at the expense of intellectuality."[40]

The scientific popularizers, then, legitimized the racist assumption that blacks were more sensual than intellectual. J. T. Virey, a French natural scientist whose writings about the Negro race were translated in 1837 and widely circulated in Charleston, wrote that "the more men and women are civilized, and cultivate their mind and intellect, the more unfit they become to propagate. Almost all the vital power is carried to the brain and senses at the expense of other organs." Thus, two white prejudices--the Negro's low intelligence and animal-like sensuality--became joined in scientific theory. Scientific racists, citing examples of masters who were unable to instill a sense of sexual morality into their slaves, generally held that blacks could never develop a moral conscience, but could only be restrained from immoral acts by their masters.[41]

The earliest explorers in Africa generated the stereotype of the blacks' lascivious nature, based on the Africans' partial nudity and sometimes polygamous social organization. Jordan documents claims by English explorers that African men had huge sexual organs and women oversized breasts.[42] Such sexual fantasies about blacks are still exhibited by whites in twentieth-century America.[43]

Racists in the antebellum South repeated the earlier

explorers' accounts of the Africans' bizarre sexual rites and excessive promiscuity. A supposed heightened sexuality was ascribed to the Negroes' sensuality as ruling their intellect. On one level, whites derided the blacks' supposed libidinous nature as evidence that blacks were closer to the brutes than whites. Yet, the existence of mulattoes in the United States evidences a white responsiveness to the "passionate race." The "natural lewdness of the negro" not only justified black subordination, but also excused miscegenation in a society where it was regarded as a serious offense against nature. Virey, for example, wrote that the skin of black women "is as soft as velvet; they are of an exceedingly warm constitution, and seem to have concentrated in their bosoms all the fires of Africa. Hence the great power which they sometimes exert over white men even to their destruction."[44]

The institution of slavery, of course, permitted unscrupulous masters to take sexual advantage of their women slaves, who, as Kenneth Stampp has shown, "were rarely in a position to freely accept or reject the advances of white men." The planters, however, either failed to see or did not question too deeply the peculiar institution's effects on the black community. The women who were forced to have intercourse with their masters or their masters' sons were especially victimized; the men who could not protect their women were dehumanized; husbands and wives could never be assured that they would not be separated from each other by sale. Even though few Southerners defended the planter's moral right to break up slave marriages, and even though Southern reformers attempted to pass legislation to curtail such practices, no Southern state enacted comprehensive laws to prevent the violation of slaves' marriages. The vast majority of planters were no doubt sincere in wanting to protect their own slaves' marriage vows, but insolvency and death too frequently resulted in the destruction of slave families. Economics, in this case, proved more powerful than moral sensibilities. The institution of slavery, then, hardly helped encourage blacks to maintain the sexual standards of white society, standards that whites too often failed to meet.[45]

Similarly, the institution of slavery also affected whites' judgment of the mental inferiority of blacks. Not only did the Southern states pass laws against teaching the slaves to read or write, but there were no economic incentives for black slaves to improve their position in society through education. Nor was it unusual for slaves to feign stupidity in order to fool their masters. Although such deception helped slaves to survive their bondage, it also reinforced white stereotypes about the inherent inferiority of blacks.[46]

The white Southerners' racist picture of blacks as sensuous and mentally dull formed the basis for several conflicting white stereotypes about black slaves on the plantation. Were the blacks carefree and mirthful Sambos even in serious situations? Their feeble minds served as an explanation. Were they terrifying and dangerous rebels? Crazy abolitionists like John Brown could easily lead them to folly by preying on their lack of judgment.[47]

The Ham story provided a valuable biblical bridge not only for justifying the enslavement of blacks in terms of divine providence, but also for explaining the inherent character of blacks. The story-tellers incorporated racist stereotypes into the story by variously interpreting the particular nature of Ham's original sin. While they all agreed that Ham had been extremely disrespectful of his father, they frequently embellished the incident of Ham's seeing Noah naked. Frederick Dalcho, an Episcopalian clergyman in Charleston, wrote, "It is probable, from the severity of the malediction, that Ham and Canaan spoke of their father's situation, with ridicule and contempt, rather than reverence and regret; while Shem and Japheth, showed their modesty and filial respect, by covering him from shame."[48]

Many proslavery writers hinted that the sin was somehow sexual in nature. Stringfellow called the sin "beastly wickedness." Nathan Lord called Ham's act an "unnatural crime" that represented his "obscene" nature. Sloan mentioned Ham's "indecency." John Fletcher claimed that Ham had sinned by marrying a daughter of the race of Cain before boarding the ark. He attempted to prove that the mark on Cain was "blackness" and that Ham therefore violated one of God's basic laws against miscegenation. Priest speculated that Ham's real "lascivious" crime was incest with his own mother. Whatever the actual crime entailed, all the commentators agreed on its wicked and impious character.[49]

Ham's sinful act was presumably indicative of his character. In the words of Stringfellow, "Ham's character is a true type of the character of his descendants" just as Jews are noted for their "reverence for the true God" and Caucasians are known for their intelligence and enterprise.[50] From a critical point of view, the modern reader can see that the expositors were reading their own racist presuppositions about blacks and whites into the story of Ham and Noah. In the process, however, a myth developed, with Ham and Japheth symbolizing Southern racist assumptions about the nature of the black and white races. Although the reasoning is quite circular, the biblical "constitution" now sustained and consolidated the former racist presuppositions that blacks were lazy and mirthful (Ham had been disrespectful to his father), superstitious and idolatrous (Ham's act was impious and wicked), and lewd and sensual (Ham's act was of a sexual nature). Perhaps Priest best combined these various themes on the relation of Ham's sin to the character of the black race:

> But in addition to what is already said respecting the Hebrew word _Ham_, we may remark that it was, in some sense, also prophetic of Ham's character and fortunes in his _own_ life, and the fortunes of his _race_, as the word not only signified _black_ in its literal sense, but pointed out the very disposition of his mind. The word, doubtless, has more meanings than we are _now_ acquainted with, _two_ of which, however, besides the first, we find are _heat_ or _violence_ of temper, exceedingly prone to acts of ferocity and cruelty, involving murder, war, butcheries, and even _cannibalism_, including beastly lusts, and lasciviousness in its _worst_ feature, going beyond the force of these passions, as possessed in common by the other races of men. Second, the word signifies deceit, dishonesty, treachery, low mindedness, and malice.
>
> What a group of horrors are here, couched in the word _Ham_, all agreeing in a most surprising manner with the color of Ham's skin, as well as with his real character as a _man_, during his own life, as well as with that of his race, even now.[51]

## The Perpetual Child

The story of Ham as narrated by American storytellers included, then, both racist stereotypes and the patriarchal ideal. Thus the story came to reflect one of the prime ambiguities in the proslavery thought of white antebellum Southerners. Were blacks a dangerous element in the society that might engulf the South in bloodshed or were they contented members of happy patriarchal families? White

Southerners could never quite decide, in part because of conflicting experiences. The slaves, who had no legal standing in the society, frequently appealed to their masters to protect them from overseers, patrollers, and slave traders. They were particularly successful when they reinforced their masters' self-image as benevolent patriarchs. Historians have interpreted the slaves' attitudes both as outright posturing for the sake of survival and as genuine signs of affection. Eugene Genovese presents some evidence to support both views. The slaves at times were certainly feigning for their own survival; at other times they did show some genuine feelings of loyalty and even affection for their masters' families.[52] In the white Southerners' mythic world, however, these expressions of loyalty by blacks evidenced not only their satisfaction with their masters' benevolence but even contentment with the institution of slavery itself.

The planters could not, however, ignore the numerous incidents that showed the slaves' discontent. They knew that slaves on other plantations had murdered their masters and overseers and had even resorted to arson. They suppressed the evidence of their own slaves' discontent, at least partially because they really believed that they were benevolent patriarchs. Their journals frequently expressed shock and even anger when one of their favorite and well-treated slaves had proven "ungrateful" and had run away. Perhaps their anger was not only directed against the runaways but also expressed fears that they had somehow failed the patriarchal ideal. Even in these instances some planters failed to recognize the blacks' desire for freedom. Louis Manigault, a large rice planter on the South Carolina coast, for example, wrote in his diary that desertions of the "House Servants" during the early days of the war convinced him that the "only suitable occupation for the Negro is to be a Labourer of the Earth."[53] Manigault was exchanging an attitude of benevolent patriarch for that of a hard-nosed racist.

The scientific racists had much earlier pictured the blacks as semi-animals, lacking all moral senses. But Southern Christians did not agree. Clergymen in the South had always insisted that the planters should encourage their slaves' conversion to Christianity. The planters generally allowed and even supported missionary activity on their plantations. If masters hoped that Christianity would make the blacks more loyal and hard-working slaves, they also had to recognize the possibility of their moral improvement. Clergymen in particular denied that the blacks' moral laxity was intrinsic. They did, however, agree with the scientific racists that native Africans lacked moral development; they also generally admitted that the blacks' lack of intelligence and imitative nature often led them into immorality. Slaves were thought to be particularly dangerous because they lacked good judgment and abolitionists might incite them to violence.

The clergymen, however, always insisted that blacks could become good Christians. For example, Frederick A. Ross, a "new school" Presbyterian minister from Huntsville, Alabama, believed that Southern masters had a great God-given responsibility to convert blacks to Christianity:

> For God has intrusted to them [the masters] to train millions of the most degraded in form and intellect, but, at the same time, the most gentle, the most amiable, the most affectionate, the most imitative, the most susceptible of social and religious love, of all the races of mankind,--to train them, and to give them civilization, and the light and the life of the gospel of Jesus Christ. And I thank God he has given this great work to that type of the noble family of Japheth best qualified to do it,--to the Cavalier stock,--the gentleman and the lady of England and France, born to command, and softened and refined under our Southern sky.[54]

Thomas Smyth wrote that polygenesis was a particularly dangerous theory not only because it attacked a literal reading of the Bible, but also because it uncharitably degraded blacks to the level of brutes. He insisted that blacks had the same moral nature as whites and were equally susceptible to Christianity.[55]

Augustin Verot, the Catholic bishop of Georgia and East Florida, followed a middle path, holding that black Christians usually lived moral lives if supervised by prudent Christian masters, yet believing that nature had endowed Negroes with weaker moral sentiments than whites. He maintained that slave owners who separated husbands and wives by sale were guilty of encouraging sexual immorality since the black "race was more inclined to pleasures than any other." Blacks could not attain continency since "the strength and violence of animal propensities is in the inverse ratio of intellectual and moral faculties, which are decidedly weaker in the African race, as all persons of experience will testify."[56]

The image of blacks as perpetual children was particularly common among the Christian racists who were trying to find a middle ground between their belief that Negroes could develop a high moral sense when Christianized and their belief in the blacks' predisposition to sensuality. Thornton Stringfellow, a Baptist minister in Virginia, wrote that "The age twenty-one, which gives bodily maturity to both races develops moral and intellectual manhood in the white race, while the African remains at the end of time, a mere child in intellectual and moral development, perfectly incapable of performing the great functions of social life."[57] This image of blacks as perpetual children helped explain seemingly inconsistent white racial attitudes: basically gentle and carefree, blacks lacked the intellectual foresight to restrain their love of pleasure, and thus could be easily tempted to lie and steal. Like children, they were taken to be generally superstitious and particularly predisposed to idolatry, yet susceptible to Christianity if proper supervision channeled beliefs in ghosts, spirits, and demons into constructive religion.

The stereotype of blacks as perpetual children came as close as possible to reconciling the slaveholder's self-image as grand patriarch with his racist beliefs. When God ordained patriarchal servitude to control the descendants of Ham, he established the perfect institution for checking their natural tendency to laziness, superstition, and crime. Proslavery writers argued that slavery had improved the moral character of blacks immensely when compared with their condition in Africa. Christianity had superseded heathenism and immorality; a mild form of servitude had supplanted a harsh form of slavery, which included cannibalism and other atrocities; sufficient food, clothing, and shelter had replaced starvation and misery. Southern literature with hardly an exception reinforced the racist stereotype of the happy slave. One early expression of the stereotype is from Thomas R. R. Cobb's Inquiry into the Law of Negro Slavery:

> The negroes thus imported were generally contented and happy.... In truth their situation when properly treated was improved by the change. Careless and mirthful by nature, they were eager to find a master when they reached the shore, and the cruel separations to which they were sometimes exposed, and which for the moment gave them excruciating agony, were forgotten at the sound of their rude musical instruments and in the midst of

> their noisy dances. The great Architect had framed them both physically and mentally to fill the sphere in which they were thrown, and His wisdom and mercy combined in constituting them thus suited to the degraded position they were destined to occupy. Hence, their submissiveness, their obedience, and their contentment.[58]

While Cobb's characterization of blacks fits the stereotype of the contented slave, George Sawyer, a prominent Louisiana lawyer and slaveholder, presented a more fearful image. He wrote that the blacks' lack of intelligence and "preponderance of the animal propensities" predisposed the slaves to all sorts of immorality, unless they were carefully controlled. Normally, according to Sawyer, "the height of his [the black's] aspirations is to satiate his appetite, then to lounge, sleep, sweat and steam in the sun, like the moping alligator upon his log by the river bank."[59]

The planters' image of blacks as perpetual children could cover the stereotypes of both the submissive slave and the moping alligator. For although the whites thought the slaves were generally carefree, lazy, and insouciant, they believed them to be especially dangerous if unrestrained because blacks had the strength of adults but only the intelligence and judgment of children. Therefore, a system of control approximating that of parental authority over children especially suited them. Samuel A. Cartwright, a physician and flamboyant defender of slavery, wrote that blacks resembled children because "they are very easily governed by love combined with fear, and are ungovernable, vicious and rude under any other form of government whatever, not resting on love and fear as a basis." Cartwright, probably tongue-in-cheek, coined the word drapetomania for "the disease causing Negroes to run away." Fortunately this "disease of the mind" was "much more curable" than most other mental diseases. Whites must only realize that it is against the divine decree either "to raise him [the black] to a level" of equality or to abuse "the power which God has given him over his fellow man."[60]

Cartwright understood the psychology of enslavement better than his extravagant metaphor of disease would suggest. Evidence shows that a vast majority of slaves who sought freedom in the North had been taught to read and write or had been especially trusted house-servants. Frederick Douglass explained the human yearning poignantly:

> Beat and cuff the slave, keep him hungry and spiritless, and he will follow the chain of his master like a dog, but feed and clothe him well, work him moderately and surround him with physical comfort, and dreams of freedom will intrude. Give him a bad master and he aspires a good master; give him a good master, and he wishes to become his own master. Such is human nature.[61]

Of course, other slaves who had extremely brutal masters tried to escape out of desperation. Basically, according to Cartwright, planters had to understand that blacks should be governed as children with both fear and love. However, just as fathers held different standards for punishing their own children, planters too had different notions about how frequently and severely their slaves should be whipped. Even if there were no exact formula for controlling slaves, white overseers, like good parents, were expected to understand the slaves' psychology and easily manage them. Perhaps this helps explain the curious phenomenon of white masters' dismissing the hired overseers after the slaves complained of mistreatment. It may not be that the masters always believed the slaves, but they certainly believed that their overseers lacked the wise patriarchal judgment necessary for easily governing the blacks.

In such a manner, the story of Ham helped to maintain both this patriarchal theory of government and racist attitudes about black inferiority. The story-tellers insisted that God's eternal decree was not only punishment for Ham's sin, but more importantly was a merciful decree "for the good of the Canaanite race," as Solon Robinson, a prominent agricultural reformer, wrote. "The excesses of his animality are kept in restraint and he is compelled to lead an industrious, sober life, and certainly a more happy one than he would if he was left to the free indulgences of his indolent, savage nature."[62] Another exponent of the Ham story wrote that the character traits of Ham's descendants "fit them for the important place ... though a subordinate one, that God intended they should occupy." Far from being cursed by the decree, "the posterity of Ham, in living among the whites and rendering service to them ... have an enhanced degree of health, length of life, comfort, security, quietness, freedom from care, and a participation in the blessings of the Gospel."[63]

## NOTES

[1]John Caldwell Calhoun, The Works, ed. Richard K. Crallé, 6 vols. (1851-1856; New York: D. Appleton, 1888), II, 630-31, V, 205.

[2]Hinton Rowan Helper, The Impending Crisis of the South, ed. George M. Fredrickson (1857; Cambridge, Mass.: Belknap Press of Harvard University, 1968), p. ix, and passim. Fredrickson's introduction to this edition explores the relationship between Helper's views on slavery and his racism. Helper's two post-Civil War books were Nojoque (New York: George W. Carleton, 1867) and The Negroes in Negroland (New York: George W. Carleton, 1868).

[3]Joseph Clarke Robert, The Road from Monticello (1941; rpt. New York: AMS, 1970), pp. 20-36 and passim; Theodore M. Whitfield, Slavery Agitation in Virginia 1829-1832 (Baltimore: Johns Hopkins, 1930), ch. 4; Charles S. Sydnor, The Development of Southern Sectionalism 1819-1848, vol. V of A History of the South, ed. W. H. Stephenson and E. M. Coulter (Baton Rouge: Louisiana State University Press, 1948), pp. 226-28; and Clement Eaton, The Growth of Southern Civilization 1790-1860 (New York: Harper and Brothers, 1961), pp. 302-3.

[4]Winthrop D. Jordan, White over Black (1968; rpt. Baltimore: Penguin Books, 1969), p. 80. Chapter 2 of this work thoroughly explores the origin of slavery in America. See also Hilrie Shelton Smith, In His Image but ... (Durham, N.C.: Duke University Press, 1972), pp. 3-4; and Edmund S. Morgan, American Slavery American Freedom (New York: W. W. Norton, 1975), chs. 15 and 16.

[5]Jordan, chs. 1 and 2.

[6]Thomas Jefferson, Notes on the State of Virginia, intro. Thomas Perkins Abernethy (1861; New York: Harper Torchbook, 1964), pp. 132-38; and Jordan, p. 455 and passim. Chapter 12 of Jordan's work explores Jefferson's thoughts about slavery and prejudice, relating them to his psychological character and his practice. See also David Brion Davis, The Problem of Slavery in the Age of Revolution 1770-1823 (Ithaca, N.Y.: Cornell University Press, 1975), pp. 169-84.

[7]Jordan, pp. 533-34; see also Richard H. Colfax,

Evidence against the Views of the Abolitionists (New York: James T. M. Bleakley, 1833), pp. 8-24.

[8]George M. Fredrickson, Black Image in the White Mind (1971; New York: Harper Torchbooks, 1972), pp. 33-42.

[9]Frederick Douglass, Life and Times of Frederick Douglass (1892; New York: Bonanza Books, 1962), p. 257.

[10]Thomas Roderick Dew, "Professor Dew on Slavery," The Pro-Slavery Argument (1852; rpt. New York: Negro Universities Press, 1968), pp. 287-89, 307-8, 328, 422, 429, 435-37. See also Fredrickson, pp. 44-46. I have drawn heavily on the second chapter of Fredrickson's excellent historical study, showing the development of racist thought and its connection with proslavery theory.

[11]William Gilmore Simms, "The Morals of Slavery," Pro-Slavery Argument, p. 269; Thornton Stringfellow, Slavery (New York: J. F. Trow, 1861), p. 4; and Thomas R. R. Cobb, An Inquiry into the Law of Negro Slavery (1858; rpt. New York: Negro Universities Press, 1968), p. 28.

[12]William Stanton, The Leopard's Spots (Chicago: University of Chicago Press, 1960), p. 194. Fredrickson, pp. 76ff., also disagrees with Stanton's conclusion that the polygenists had no impact on racism in the South.

[13]John H. Van Evrie, Negroes and Negro "Slavery" (3rd ed., 1863; rpt. Miami: Mnemosyne, 1969), pp. 23, 37, 53, 55. See also George S. Sawyer, Southern Institutes (1859; rpt. Miami: Mnemosyne, 1969), p. 163; L. S. M., "Negromania," De Bow's Review 12 (May 1852), 508; and George Fitzhugh, "The Black and White Races of Men," De Bow's Review 30 (April 1861), 448.

[14]Josiah Clark Nott, Two Lectures on the Connection between the Biblical and Physical History of Man (1849; rpt. New York: Negro Universities Press, 1969), p. 20.

[15]Wilson Carey McWilliams, The Idea of Fraternity in America (Berkeley: University of California, 1973), p. 258.

[16]Jordan, pp. 4-20.

[17]Jefferson, p. 133.

[18]John Woolman, "Some Considerations on the Keeping of Negroes," Journal and Essays of John Woolman, ed. Amelia M. Gummere (1774; New York: Macmillan, 1922), pp. 366-68.

[19]David Rice, "Racial Mixture and Slavery," Racial Thought in America, Vol. I, From the Puritans to Abraham Lincoln, ed. Louis Ruchames (New York: Universal Library, Grosset & Dunlap, 1970), pp. 226-27.

[20]Dew, p. 447.

[21]Van Evrie, pp. v, 90, 168. See also Samuel Adolphus Cartwright, "Diseases and Peculiarities of the Negro Race, part 3," De Bow's Review 11 (Sept. 1851), 331-36; Josiah Clark Nott, An Essay on the Natural History of Mankind (Mobile, Ala.: Dade, Thompson, 1851), p. 19; and Josiah Clark Nott, "Statistics of Southern Slave Population," De Bow's Review 4 (Nov. 1847), 284.

[22]Cartwright, "Diseases," p. 66.

[23]Samuel Adolphus Cartwright, "How to Save the Republic, and the Position of the South in the Union," De Bow's Review 11 (Aug. 1851), 184; and Samuel Adolphus Cartwright, "Dr. Cartwright on the Caucasians and the Africans," De Bow's Review 25 (July 1858), 47.

[24]Cartwright, "Diseases," pp. 68-69. See also Cartwright, "How to Save the Republic," p. 186.

[25]Fitzhugh, p. 453.

[26]James A. Sloan, The Great Question Answered (Memphis: Hutton, Gallaway, 1857), pp. 78-81.

[27]Cartwright, "Diseases," p. 68.

[28]Sloan, p. 78.

[29]Iveson L. Brookes, A Defence of the South (Hamburg, S. C.: The Republican Office, 1850), p. 23. See also [Iveson L. Brookes], A Defence of Southern Slavery (Hamburg, S.C.: Robinson and Carlisle, 1851), p. 6.

[30]African Servitude (New York: Davies & Kent, 1860), pp. 10, 16.

[31]Josiah Priest, Slavery (Albany, N.Y.: C. Van Benthuysen, 1843), pp. 15, 27-28.

[32]Leander Ker, Slavery Consistent with Christianity, 3rd ed. (Weston, Mo.: Finch and O'Gorman, Reporter Office, 1853), pp. iii, 11-13, 29-30. The first edition was in 1838.

Ker's claim to have been the first to give a public defense of slavery based on the Bible is doubtful, since there were already several written defenses of slavery based primarily on the Bible by 1838. See for example [Frederick Dalcho], Practical Considerations Founded on the Scriptures (Charleston, S.C.: A. E. Miller, 1823).

[33]Ker, p. 10.

[34]Priest, p. 33.

[35]John Bachman, The Doctrine of the Unity of the Human Race (Charleston, S.C.: C. Canning, 1850), p. 212.

[36]Thomas Smyth, The Unity of the Human Races (1851), in Complete Works of Rev. Thomas Smyth, D.D., ed. J. William Flinn, 10 vols. (Columbia, S.C.: R. L. Bryan, 1910), VIII, 249.

[37][Patrick H. Mell], Slavery (Penfield, Ga.: Benj. Brantley, 1844), p. 37. See also Frederick Augustus Ross, Slavery Ordained of God (1857; rpt. Miami: Mnemosyne, 1969), p. 67.

[38]J. Aitken Meigs, "The Cranial Characteristics of the Races of Man," Indigenous Races of the Earth, ed. Josiah C. Nott and George R. Gliddon (Philadelphia: J. B. Lippincott, 1857), pp. 203-352. Meigs was Morton's student who helped him classify the skulls; he presented the summary of their studies in this work. Josiah Clark Nott and George R. Gliddon, Types of Mankind (Philadelphia: Lippincott, Grambo, 1854), p. 450; Nott, "Statistics," p. 280; Nott, Two Lectures, pp. 35-38; Van Evrie, pp. 63, 123-31; Cobb, pp. 25-36; Samuel Adolphus Cartwright, "Diseases and Peculiarities of the Negro Race, Part 1," De Bow's Review 11 (July 1851), 65; and Matthew Estes, A Defense of Negro Slavery (Montgomery: Press of the "Alabama Journal," 1846), pp. 50-52, 66-67.

[39]Cobb, pp. 30-35. See also Estes, pp. 66-67; Van

Evrie, pp. 123-31, 228; Sawyer, pp. 198-99; and J. H. Guenebault, ed., Natural History of the Negro Race (Charleston, S.C.: D. J. Dowling, 1837), pp. 1-3, 5.

[40]Cartwright, "Diseases..., Part 1," pp. 65-66.

[41]Guenebault, pp. 94-97; William Harper, "Harper on Slavery," Pro-Slavery Argument, p. 59.

[42]Jordan, pp. 32-39; 136-78.

[43]Joel Kovel, White Racism (New York: Vintage Books, 1971), pp. 63-82 and passim; Gunnar Myrdal, An American Dilemma, 2 vols. (New York: Harper & Brothers, 1944), I, 55-57, 59-60, 586-87, 589-92; II, 1355-56; and John Dollard, Caste and Class in a Southern Town, 3rd ed. (1937; New York: Doubleday Anchor Books, 1949), pp. 134-72.

[44]Guenebault, pp. 88-89; Cobb, pp. ccxix, 40; Sawyer, p. 196; Helper, Negroes, pp. 75-78, 105-17; and John Fletcher, Studies on Slavery (Natchez, Miss.: Jackson Warner, 1852), pp. 38-39, 138-55, 198.

[45]Kenneth M. Stampp, The Peculiar Institution (1956; New York: Alfred A. Knopf, 1968), pp. 350-61 and passim; Eugene Genovese, Roll Jordan Roll (1972; New York: Vintage Books of Random House, 1976), pp. 413-431 includes a particularly sensitive account of miscegenation, exploring both genuine loving relationships that sometimes transcended racism and also the exploitation of blacks in many more of the relationships; see also John W. Blassingame, The Slave Community (New York: Oxford University, 1972), pp. 81-85 and passim.

[46]Stampp, pp. 97-109.

[47]See especially Blassingame, ch. 5 and passim.

[48]Dalcho, p. 9.

[49]Sloan, pp. 66-67; Priest, pp. 152-53; Fletcher, pp. 248-54, 437-40, 443-64; Stringfellow, p. 12; and Nathan Lord, A Northern Presbyter's Second Letter (Boston: Little, Brown, 1855), pp. 42, 57.

[50]Stringfellow, p. 35.

[51]Priest, p. 33.

[52]Genovese explores the white Southerners' conflicting picture of their black slaves in Part I of Roll Jordan Roll.

[53]Quoted in Genovese, p. 101; see also pp. 97-112.

[54]Ross, pp. 67-68.

[55]Smyth, pp. 75, 141, 147-48, 249, 338-44.

[56]Augustin Verot, A Tract for the Times (New Orleans: n.p., 1861), p. 12. See also Mell, p. 37; Dalcho, pp. 6, 19; William A. Smith, Lectures on the Philosophy and Practice of Slavery (Nashville: Stevenson & Evans, 1856), pp. 170-71; and Sloan, p. 291.

[57]Stringfellow, pp. 4, 10. See also Dew, p. 449; Cartwright, "Diseases..., Part 1," p. 67; and George Fitzhugh, Sociology for the South (1854; rpt. New York: Burt Franklin, [1965]), pp. 82-83.

[58]Cobb, pp. clvi-clvii. See also Harper, p. 19; Fletcher, p. 199; Sawyer, pp. 201-2; Estes, pp. 96-139; William J. Grayson, "The Hireling and the Slave," De Bow's Review 21 (Sept. 1856), 251-52; and Robert Lewis Dabney, A Defense of Virginia (1867; rpt. New York: Negro Universities Press, 1969), p. 281.

[59]Sawyer, p. 196; see also Cobb, pp. 36-41; Guenebault, pp. 3, 5, 29; Nott, "Statistics," p. 279; Estes, pp. 52-60; Helper, Negroes, passim; and Dabney, pp. 279-80.

[60]Cartwright, "Diseases..., Part 1," p. 67; and Cartwright, "Diseases..., Part 3," pp. 331-32.

[61]Douglass, p. 150.

[62]Solon Robinson, "Negro Slavery at the South," De Bow's Review 7 (Sept. 1849), 212.

[63]African Servitude, p. 15.

## Chapter V

# JAPHETH, HAM, AND SHEM IN AMERICA

An anonymous writer in the Southern Literary Messenger declared that "for the first time, the white man, the black man, and the red man stood face to face, and gazed upon each other in the New World." The relationship among these three races in America was fulfilling "that remarkable prophecy uttered thousands of years before by the Patriarch Noah, when standing upon the mount of inspiration, and looking down the course of future time, he proclaimed: 'God shall enlarge Japheth, and he shall dwell in the tents of Shem, and Canaan shall be his servant.'"[1] As the story of Noah and his three sons came to be part of the sacred history of the American nation, it clearly functioned as a cultural myth. Ham, Japheth, and Shem became the archetypes for the black, white, and red races coexisting in America. How did the story fit the enslavement of blacks into the American dream of manifest destiny? Was the story widespread enough in the Old South to function as a cultural myth?

### Japheth's Mission

The early Puritans had believed themselves to be God's chosen people in the wilderness and interpreted their experiences as analogous to those of the ancient Hebrews. They were building the kingdom of God on earth, hoping that God would establish his rule in America. During the revolutionary period the ideals of civil liberty, of representative government, and of constitutional rights came to be joined to the earlier Christian hopes in the American imagination. Americans began to view themselves as the political beacon of light to the rest of the world. In the first half of the nineteenth century the westward expansion convinced many that God had destined America to become a great nation that would be a religious and political model for the rest of the world.

Yet the issue of slavery marred this happy vision by driving a wedge between North and South. Abolitionists challenged the morality of Southern society and claimed that the Southern social order represented neither the civil nor the religious ideals of the American nation. For Southerners, the story of Noah and his three sons became particularly persuasive because it could so easily join the enslavement of blacks to the manifest destiny of whites in America. Samuel Davies Baldwin, a Methodist minister in Tennessee, dramatically wove the image that America was God's chosen nation into the Ham myth:

> Christianity was promised, and she stood by the Constitution; Liberty was promised, and she stood by Christianity; Knowledge was promised, and she walked forth with Liberty; Progress was promised, and her stormy chariot thundered when Washington was sworn; the tents of Shem were promised, and the eagle spread its wings over America; honor was promised, and stars of glory spangled the new-born firmament; power was promised, and stripes for the nations swept the air; service was promised, and Canaan ministered at Japheth's feet; dominion was promised and the prescient oracles echoed 'from sea to sea, and from _the river_ to the ends of the earth.'[2]

Christians in the antebellum South, like their Puritan ancestors, believed that a hidden meaning lay behind everyday occurrences. Coincidence and chance were not acceptable explanations for the events of history; nor were completely naturalistic ones. God's mysterious hand somehow guided human actions as well as natural events. Howell Cobb, a governor of Georgia and Speaker of the United States House of Representatives, insisted that God's care was "manifested in every circumstance and event, over and above all human sagacity and prudence." If one carefully searched the Scriptures and piously examined events, one might begin to understand the divine purpose or the providence of God. Cobb, like other white Southerners who sought the religious significance behind the enslavement of blacks in America, found some clues about God's design in Genesis 9.[3]

An anonymous essay in the _Southern Literary Messenger_ that may have been written by George Tucker, a prominent literary figure in Virginia who served as a United States congressman and held a chair in moral philosophy at the University of Virginia, explored God's purpose in permitting blacks to be enslaved in America. The author, who claimed to be a "philosophic historian," believed that the events surrounding the birth of the American nation could "furnish the solution" to "this vexed question" for "those who know how to read" these events correctly. What was the solution? The author theorized that God permitted black slavery in order to further the cause of civil and religious liberty in the world. When the Dutch ship first brought its unsought cargo of slaves to Virginia, God's holy people was besieged on all sides. England could not protect the colonists against the hostility of France and Spain nor against that of the Indians. The vastly outnumbered colonists survived only through the blessings of God's providence. Americans had many tasks to perform if they were to be successful. They had to repel the European military forces, subdue the Indians, and claim and settle the land in order to wrest it from Catholic Spain and France. Had the new nation been left alone in peace, it might have become a free country based on popular institutions without developing the anomalous institution of black slavery. Under the circumstances, however, if the work could not be accomplished quickly, the holy experiment would be doomed at the start. The importation of Africans, the sons of Ham, to serve Japheth in this great mission was a gift of God, showing his support for the British colonies.[4]

The author invented a conversation between the most intelligent representative of Ham's race and a representative of Japheth to express this theme when the whites first subordinated the Africans in America. In order that Ham would understand his position in the new nation, Japheth tells him that

> 'Our races are different; so different that even good Christians are loath to believe that we are both descended from the same pair. We also have lately come across the broad water, but from the most Western Isles of the Land of Japhet, whither our fathers came from the far, far East. Their journeyings, vicissitudes and discipline of more than a thousand years, through peace and war, have made us what you see us. We are here now under the auspices and protection of our fatherland. But something whispers us that we have come for other purposes than to promote our own

> separate interest or that of our king. It may be that we are to found a new empire. It may be that the fortunes of those we left behind us are bound up with our adventure, and to conduct this to a safe issue may require the highest qualities of human nature. The mighty plan, though now dimly seen by the wisest, will be developed in time. A great though unknown work lies before our posterity whom we must train for the duty as our fathers trained us. Meantime we know surely that yonder forest is first to be subdued and the soil reclaimed for the use of man. In this you might participate: for this you may have been sent to us by the Great Being who rules and guides us all.'[5]

Ham accepts the principle of subordination and agrees to serve Japheth in his mission:

> 'Sons of Japhet and children of the white man, you know why we are here. We came not willingly, but we charge not our captivity to you. Yet here we are and we submit to our lot. It may have been for our sins or those of our fathers that we are torn from our native land; but better is it thus than that our race should have been cut off as cumberers of the earth. A long and fearful penance may be before us, but bitterer it cannot be than the oppression we have left behind.... A great mission you say, awaits you. In our hearts we can believe it true. And something whispers us that we also, all fallen as we are, have a duty to perform in connexion therewith. We ask not to be admitted to your higher sphere. Would that we were worthy.'[6]

Ham then asks that he be properly fed, housed, and clothed and that his "perverseness" be corrected "until the curse is removed from our race." He will gladly serve the white man in his task of claiming and settling the land as long as his basic physical needs and moral instruction in the gospel are met, hoping in the meantime that God will eventually lead him back to Africa as a new man to reward him for his service of helping to establish a new godly nation.[7]

This remarkable dialogue between Ham and Japheth fit the whites' racial beliefs and institution of slavery into the Southerners' religious universe. By framing the blacks' subordination in terms of God's plan for America, the story depicted a sacred history and therefore clearly functioned as a religious myth. A story becomes mythic when it makes everyday attitudes and motivations fit a universal context. Thus, racist attitudes in the antebellum South were not "religious" simply because they were deeply held, but because they were enclosed in a universal system of belief (world view) that gave meaning to the nature and destiny of the white race in America, the New Israel. In the version of the Ham myth quoted here, God has allowed Ham's bondage in order to fulfill a divine purpose rather than to further Japheth's personal interests or those of any human government. Japheth sees his mission only dimly, uncertain whether America will become the center of a new empire or whether a spiritual rejuvenation in America will enlighten Europe. Thus, the Southerners' inherited belief from the Puritans that America was God's beacon of light to the rest of the world validated the Southerners' racial ethos by providing the context within which slavery and black subordination could be understood as part of divine destiny.

A closer examination reveals that this version of the Ham myth mediates the basic contradiction in the views of moderate racists in the antebellum South--i.e., if black Christians were brothers of the whites, then how could whites enslave blacks? While Ham and Japheth are clearly brothers in the story, blacks as a race have no right to self determination; although black bondage is not explicitly linked to Noah's curse, the enlightened son of Ham does suggest that sins committed in the past require expiation, and later he makes reference to his "fallen" state. In any case, both Ham and Japheth declare that God, not Japheth, has enslaved Ham in America: Japheth explains to Ham that "you may have been sent to us by the Great Being who rules and guides us all" in order to help physically build God's kingdom on earth; Ham responds, "We came not willingly, but we charge not our captivity to you." Ham hopes that one day God will remove "the curse" from his race when his sins have been expiated and his perversity corrected. Thus, blacks can make moral progress under the guidance of whites, but only God can lead them to freedom.

Philip Schaff, a highly respected historian of Christianity, agreed that the enslavement of the African race in America resulted from Noah's curse. He wrote that "Ham dwells in the western tents of Japheth and is trained in

America for his final deliverance from the ancient curse of bondage by the slow but sure operation of Christianity." Noah's curse "will be lifted only by the future pages of history," when God will change the "curse into a blessing." Schaff believed that "a noble mission" one day awaited the American blacks when they would become missionaries "to the entire mysterious continent of Africa." Then Noah's curse would be supplanted by the Davidic blessing in Psalm 68 that "Ethiopia shall stretch out her hands unto God."[8]

Black clergymen in the antebellum period frequently tried to find a religious meaning for their race's enslavement in America. They, too, attempted to understand the mysterious workings of divine providence. Gayraud S. Wilmore presents evidence to show that black clergymen, not infrequently, accepted their race's descent from Ham, since the Bible clearly listed Ethiopia and Egypt as Ham's descendants. Ministers who were sympathetic to black emigration and colonization, such as Martin Delany, Edward Blyden, Richard Allen, Lott Carey, James T. Holly, Henry Highland Garnet, Alexander Crummel, and Henry M. Turner, agreed with Schaff that God was preparing the black race in America to carry the Christian message back to Africa, thereby fulfilling the blessing in Psalm 68. They did, however, deny that Japheth had a prophetic right to enslave blacks, since they descended from Cush and Mizraim rather than Canaan.[9]

Schaff was alone among the white exponents of the Ham myth in suggesting that God would someday overturn Noah's curse completely. Only two other story-tellers even thought that the American slaves would be freed and colonized in Africa to govern themselves.[10] Frederick A. Ross, a "New School" Presbyterian minister in Huntsville, Alabama, thought that slavery would one day end with the children of Ham returning to Africa: "I see," he wrote, "the African crossing as certainly as if I gazed upon the ocean divided by a great wind.... There is the black man's home." However, while Ham "will rise in the Christian grandeur to be revealed," God decreed in Genesis 9 that he "will be ever lower than Shem; Shem will be ever lower than Japheth."[11] The other exponents of the Ham myth believed that Ham would always be subservient to Japheth. Baldwin even believed that it was Japheth's mission to enlarge himself more by exploiting the resources of Africa:

> The cultivation of Africa is a necessity of the world.... Were Africa under full agricultural and

> and mineral development, the whole earth would be richer by it: every part of Europe and America would feel the rising tide of wealth, and every purse be dilated by it.... Whether European or American Japheth is to be the overseer may yet be a question of vital interest....
>
> Subserviency of the [Hamitic] race to Japheth will continue with time, but the mode of that subserviency will not always be confined to personal bondage.[12]

According to Thornton Stringfellow, a Baptist clergyman in Virginia, God had established the future relationship between Ham and Japheth: "God announced his purpose of subordinating these nations one to another. This subordination was to harmonize with their leading traits of character, and its ultimate object was their general good." At one time slavery had been "spread over the whole globe, embracing the descendants of Shem, Ham, and Japheth"; when emancipated, however, the descendants of Shem and Japheth progressed, and reached higher attainments in freedom, while the descendants of Ham "invariably retrograded from the position they had reached under the enlightened control of Shem or Japheth. The invariable tendency of freedom was to sink them to the level of their original degradation." Thus, Genesis 9:18-27 revealed the "divine plan unfolded for controlling or governing all the subdivisions or social organizations among men."[13]

Ham and Japheth were clearly the archetypes of the black and white races who were living together in the same nation. But how does Shem fit into the myth? Shem was, of course, a relatively minor character in the antebellum South where whites were primarily interested in fixing the relationships between planters and slaves in an eternal decree. He nevertheless emerges as a significant actor in those versions of the story which emphasized Japheth's manifest destiny. Shem was the archetype for the red or brown race, which included American Indians, persons of Oriental descent, and Jews. Shem's mission was to spread the knowledge of the true God throughout the world to prepare for the Messiah's coming. Shem, in the words of Samuel Davies Baldwin, a Methodist minister in Tennessee, was to follow "the order of God, the King of nations and High-Priest of religion. He represented the authority of the God-man, Heir of heaven and of earth." In this mission "Ham was his servant by reason of transgression; Japheth was his ward, over whom he was guardian. If he failed in the discharge of the duties of his office," his "birthright prerogatives" would be forfeited. Only the Jewish nation of all the nations belonging to the race of Shem fulfilled its spiritual task of serving the true God. Therefore, God permitted the Canaanites to serve the Jews. The rest of Shem's descendants fell into idolatry and lost their birthright.[14] Both Baldwin and Samuel A. Cartwright, a prominent Southern physician, accepted the scientific hypothesis that the American Indian was the same racial type as the Oriental; the Oriental, they believed, had once crossed a northern land bridge, long since destroyed, to settle in America.[15]

Japheth replaced Shem's spiritual mission when Shem "spurned" Christianity "from his tents." According to the Baldwin version,

> Japheth alone received it as the messenger of light, and then sunk again to slumber through ages dark with dismal dreams. Providence was weary with the lassitude of man. He broke the empire of corruption at a blow.... He lifted the veil and showed him America, the birthright of Shem, and bade him inherit and enter, possess and improve. He gave him the ancient commission to coerce the race of Ham to bear its part of tribute by tilling the soil and subduing the earth. He made him observe the imbecility of Shem, and unbar his gates, break down his doors, and rouse him from narcotic visions by the thunder of his power.[16]

When Shem's mission had ended with the coming of Christ (the Jews had refused to accept him as the Messiah), it was time to fulfill the prophecy made to Japheth. He was to spread Christianity throughout the world. In the words of Stringfellow, Ham was "to serve Japheth also, while Japheth was prosecuting the great mission assigned of God to him, of developing the intellectual and material treasures of the entire globe."[17] Baldwin wrote that Japheth "is the Divinely-inaugurated president of the world, adjured to maintain its national constitution inviolable. He must place all countries under tribute," especially Ham's descendants "in Africa, Australia, and India. If Shem will not work, he must perish: if Ham will not labor, he must become Japheth's slave."[18]

Cartwright put the myth forcefully into the American context:

But how was Japheth, cooped up in Europe, the smallest division of the earth, to be enlarged? There was no room in populous Asia for him to spread, the climate of Africa was too inhospitable for him to dwell in; yet the prophecy was not a dead letter, it was to be carried out, though the means were hidden from view during thousands of years. At length, in the fulness of time, Japheth unexpectedly discovered an unknown hemisphere, thinly inhabited by the race of Shem, and hastened to take possession of it, and to dwell in the tents of Shem.... [Here Cartwright gives some evidence linking the American Indian to the Oriental race, and therefore to Shem.] By the discovery of America Japheth became enlarged, as had been foretold three thousand eight hundred years before. He took the whole continent. He literally dwelt in the tents of Shem in Mexico and South America. At this day, in our own country, he is dwelling in the wilderness, which constituted, a few years ago, the tents of Shem. No sooner did Japheth begin to enlarge himself, and to dwell in the tents of Shem, than Canaan left his fastnesses in the wilds of Africa, where the white man's foot had never trod, and appeared on the beach to get passage to America, as if drawn thither by an impulse of his nature to fulfil his destiny of becoming Japheth's servant. Japheth did not go into the wilderness and African deserts to look for Canaan and tear him from the home of his fathers. How did he get hold of Canaan? Ask the Hebrew verb from which the name of Canaan is derived and it will tell. <u>Submisit</u> <u>se</u>; Canaan <u>submitted</u> <u>himself</u>. Japheth even made him <u>servant</u> of <u>servants</u> by putting him under the delegated authority of overseers and others. Why did he not make Shem his servant after taking his tents from him? Why cross the ocean for Canaan in the wilds of Africa, when Shem was at his door? He was compelled against his will to carry out God's decree without knowing it. He tried, but he could not make a servant of Shem. God had not decreed that Shem should serve Japheth. The wealth of all Europe could not tempt the aboriginal American, the son of the renowned Shem, to sell his brethren into bondage. When forced into bondage he met death in all its forms rather than serve as a slave. Whereas, a few beads and

> trinkets set one half of the descendants of Canaan in Africa to stealing, catching and selling the other half into bondage; and when thus sold they made the most obedient and faithful slaves. Although a stormy ocean separated Japheth, in the tents of Shem in America, from Canaan, yet neither that wide waste of waters nor the inaccessible deserts and wilds of Africa could prevent the accomplishment of God's decree. Canaan came forth and became the good and faithful servant of Japheth, when he could easily, by leaguing with Shem, still powerful and lurking in hostility around the tents he had been driven from, have exterminated the race of Japheth in America. But it is contrary to the first principles of his nature for Canaan to league with his master's enemies.--He cannot do it, be they British, Indians or abolitionists. He is bound by the decree to be true to his master.[19]

In the Cartwright text the institution of slavery and white beliefs about the nature of the two other racial groups on the American continent were framed in a sacred story or myth, rooted in rather than controlled by the biblical story of Noah and his three sons. Thus, the myth allowed white Southerners to understand the destiny of America in terms of God's will. Believing themselves to be the inheritors of the religion of their American forefathers, Southerners naturally sought explanations of their universe in the Old Testament. That this explanation could so easily encompass their views about the function and purpose of government made it a viable mythic option, not only in helping them understand their destiny, but also subsequently in reinforcing their racial stereotypes.

According to Baldwin, the prophecy of Noah was fulfilled "most sublimely in America":

> It is obvious in a universal and permanent trinity of races; in their political inequality of condition; in the Christianization of all the Japhetic nations, and of no others; in the occupation of the Shemitic wilderness of America by Japheth; and in the service of Ham to Japheth in the Southern States, in the islands, and in South America.[20]

The various versions of the Ham story quoted in this section clearly functioned as myth, or story that symbolized for white Southerners their role in America and their place in the world. God intervened in the family of Noah to establish and differentiate three new races. Ham's sin and Noah's subsequent curse permanently determined the character of the black race for all time. While Shem had been blessed by Noah, his descendants failed in their mission of remaining faithful to God, and thus the birthright passed to Japheth. Ham as the archetype of the black race committed a lascivious and wicked sin, which expressed disrespect for his father. The story, therefore, legitimized the racist attitudes in the antebellum South that pictured blacks as sensuous, lazy, and mirthful, rather than intellectual and industrious. God's edict, dooming Ham's descendants to slavery, validated the South's peculiar institution; slavery allowed the inherently indolent and weak-minded race to work productively for the advancement of civilization.

Most remarkably, these versions of the Ham myth captured and symbolized the aspirations of white Southerners who believed that America was the stage for the final scene in the divine drama that would usher in a new spiritual age on earth. According to the Baldwin and Stringfellow versions of the Ham myth, the creation of the world and the first parents provided the prologue for the sacred drama. Act One included God's creation of the three primordial races of humanity, each with its own mission to fulfill--Shem was guardian of God's laws, Japheth was the custodian of the world's wealth, Ham was the menial servant. Act Two chronicled the failure of all three sons of Noah--Shem abandoned the true religion when he rejected Jesus as Messiah, Ham sank into barbarism, idolatry, and indolence, Japheth who accepted Christianity remained cooped up in Europe and flirted with papal heresies. Act Three pictured Japheth recapturing the pure biblical faith and discovering the American continent. In the final scene Japheth, Ham, and Shem encounter each other once again--Japheth drives Shem from his tents and enslaves Ham in order to build a great spiritual and materially wealthy nation.

## The Exponents of the Myth

The argument that the story of Noah and his three sons can be regarded as myth in the antebellum South rests on three criteria--function, language, and usage. The versions of the story used in this study clearly functioned as myth because the characters and their actions symbolized cultural beliefs, institutions, and attitudes. As symbols, they helped join white racial attitudes, the economic advantages of slavery, and governmental theories within the context of God's plan for America as literally revealed in the Bible. Chapter VI will analyze the story's mythic function in detail. The narrators used a particular style of language to tell the story of Noah and his three sons. This particular mythic language gave religious validity to the aspirations and fears of white Southerners in their relationship to blacks. Chapter VII will unpack the symbolic language that the storytellers used.

But the story of Ham had to be widespread and taken seriously in the antebellum South for it to be a myth. Myths are, after all, shared cultural symbols. There is no question that Ham was popularly identified as the progenitor of the black race, especially among those people who accepted the Bible as the literal word of God that to some degree prophesied future events. Even a large number of black clergymen agreed that they were descended from Ham.[21] While not all Christian racists appealed to the story of Ham in their defense of slavery, I have found only one example where a clergyman in the antebellum South unequivocally rejected Ham as the progenitor of the black race. Experiments with hybridization and domestication of animals led John Bachman, a prominent American naturalist and Lutheran pastor in Charleston, to assert environmental factors as sufficient causes for blacks and whites to have developed into "permanent varieties"; there was no need, therefore, to posit the miraculous intervention of God.[22] Robert Lewis Dabney, Virginia's leading Presbyterian theologian, suggested that Genesis 9 should not be "regarded, nor advanced, as of prime force and importance in" the proslavery argument; while there may be "little difficulty in tracing the lineage of the present Africans to Ham," lack of historical evidence made application of the biblical text to the American situation conjectural.[23]

Although one Southern clergyman repudiated the thesis that the blacks descended from Ham and a couple of others expressed reservations, white Southern Christians overwhelmingly thought that Ham was the aboriginal black man. Between 1831 and 1861 writings abound that made some allusion to the story of Noah and his three sons. The story was certainly among the most popular defenses of slavery, if not the most popular. The major exponents of the Ham myth--those whose overall arguments clearly depend on the story of Noah

(cont. on p. 105)

## OCCUPATIONS AND DENOMINATIONS OF MAJOR EXPONENTS OF THE HAM MYTH

### Non-Clerics and Their Occupations

William G. Brownlow (editor of Knoxville Whig, U.S. senator, a former Methodist minister)

Samuel A. Cartwright (physician)

Howell Cobb (governor of Georgia, Speaker of U.S. House of Representatives, president of Provisional Congress of the Confederacy)

Matthew Estes (physician and minor novelist)

John Fletcher (planter)

Reverdy Johnson (U.S. Attorney General, U.S. senator)

Josiah Priest (harness-maker)

Solon Robinson (agricultural reformer)

John B. Thrasher (lawyer)

George Tucker (congressman and professor of moral philosophy at University of Virginia) [note: Tucker's inclusion here is conjectural; see reference 4]

### Clerics and Their Denominations

Samuel D. Baldwin (Methodist)

Iveson L. Brookes (not known)

John L. Dagg (Baptist)

Frederick Dalcho (Episcopalian)

John England (Roman Catholic; a bishop)

Leander Ker (Protestant military chaplain)

Nathan Lord (Congregational)

Alexander McCaine (Methodist)

Patrick H. Mell (Baptist)

J. C. Mitchell (Presbyterian)

Frederick A. Ross (Presbyterian)

Philip Schaff (German Reformed)

James A. Sloan (Presbyterian)

Thornton Stringfellow (Baptist)

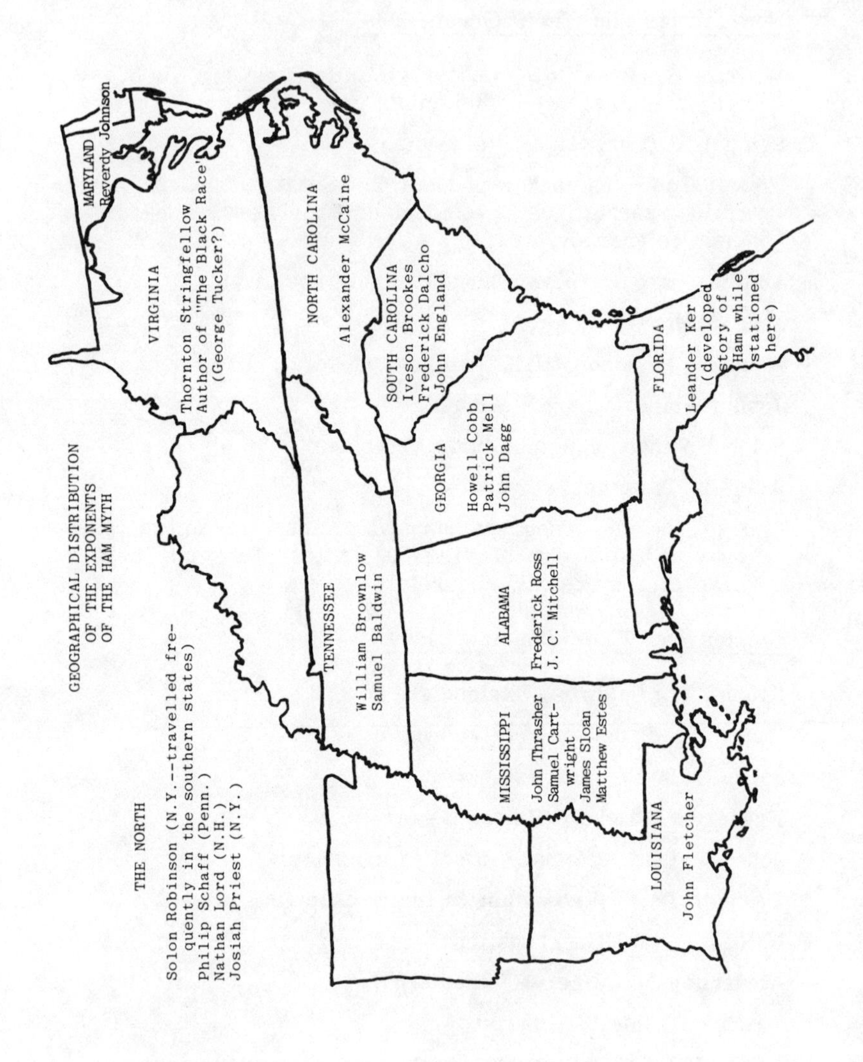
GEOGRAPHICAL DISTRIBUTION
OF THE EXPONENTS
OF THE HAM MYTH
THE NORTH
Solon Robinson (N.Y.--travelled fre-
quently in the southern states)
Philip Schaff (Penn.)
Nathan Lord (N.H.)
Josiah Priest (N.Y.)
MARYLAND
Reverdy Johnson
VIRGINIA
Thornton Stringfellow
Author of "The Black Race"
(George Tucker?)
NORTH CAROLINA
Alexander McCaine
SOUTH CAROLINA
Iveson Brookes
Frederick Dalcho
John England
GEORGIA
Howell Cobb
Patrick Mell
John Dagg
FLORIDA
Leander Ker
(developed
story of
Ham while
stationed
here)
TENNESSEE
William Brownlow
Samuel Baldwin
ALABAMA
Frederick Ross
J. C. Mitchell
MISSISSIPPI
John Thrasher
Samuel Cart-
wright
James Sloan
Matthew Estes
LOUISIANA
John Fletcher

and his three sons--include people from various professions. Clergymen represented Baptist, Presbyterian, Methodist, Episcopalian, Roman Catholic, Congregational, and German Reformed denominations. The story-tellers practiced their professions in at least nine different Southern states.[24]

These exponents of the Ham story were, for the most part, highly respected members of their professions and their communities. With the possible exceptions of the flamboyant Samuel A. Cartwright and the quixotic Josiah Priest, whose extravagant language raises a few doubts about their sincerity, the story-tellers narrated their tales with conviction. Historians, of course, can never be sure how many people were convinced by these arguments nor how many found their world a bit more comprehensible. Unlike the anthropologist who can test a story's cultural significance as a symbol system among all people in a society, the historian must select and rely on the written documents of a few. These documents, however, do demonstrate that the story of Noah's three sons functioned as myth in various geographical regions among people in different religious denominations and professions, thereby providing a viable mythic option for people in the antebellum South.

Since Southerners lived in a pluralistic culture, the myth was not, however, fully persuasive for everyone. In particular, science and history at times directly challenged the Ham myth as a factual account of racial origins. Quite naturally, ethnologists who comprised the American School rejected the story of Ham as inauthentic because their evidence tended to support polygenesis rather than literal interpretations of the Pentateuch. George Gliddon argued in *Types of Mankind* that the identification of the Negro with Ham had "the double misfortune of being physiologically and historically impossible, as well as wholly anti-biblical." He maintained that physiological differences between blacks and whites cast doubt on their descent from the same original pair, that hieroglyphic evidence from the monuments of ancient Egypt proved the "Kanani," or Canaanites, to be Caucasians, and that according to "the plain words" of Genesis 9 Canaan, rather than Ham, was cursed.[25] Significantly, the story of Noah's three sons did function as myth among Southerners who saw their society as God's New Israel and who believed that blacks were inherently inferior to whites. The Ham myth came increasingly to be a model not only *of* what white Southerners believed, but also *for* their believing it.[26]

NOTES

[1]"Africa in America," Southern Literary Messenger 22 (Jan. 1856), 1; see also Thornton Stringfellow, Slavery (New York: J. F. Trow, 1861), pp. 34-35.

[2]Samuel Davies Baldwin, Dominion; or, The Unity and Trinity of the Human Race (Nashville: E. Stevenson and F. A. Owen, 1857), pp. 389-390.

[3]Howell Cobb, A Scriptural Examination of the Institution of Slavery in the United States (1856; rpt. New York: Books for Libraries Press, 1972), pp. 6-8, 25-31.

[4]"The Black Race in North America; Why Was Their Introduction Permitted?," Southern Literary Messenger 21 (Nov. 1855), 646-47 and passim. The editor of the Southern Literary Messenger wrote that the article's "elegance of style and the clearness of the demonstration" made it an extremely important one. The article was subsequently republished in three installments in De Bow's Review 20 (Jan.-March 1856), 1-21, 190-214, 290-315. De Bow remarked that he was publishing the article even though he disagreed with the author's belief that colonization would one day remove the black race from America. It was uncommon for the two most important Southern journals to publish the same article.

I think that George Tucker is very likely the author of this anonymous article. The ideas in this essay all correspond with those of Tucker--e.g., the correlation of slavery with population density, slavery's eventual demise through colonization, the progress of civilization, etc. The author identifies himself as a Virginian and there are several stylistic similarities in this essay with those authored by George Tucker. See particularly, George Tucker, The History of the United States, from Their Colonization to the End of the Twenty-Sixth Congress, in 1841, 4 vols. (Philadelphia: J. B. Lippincott & Co., 1856-1858). For Tucker's ideas, see Robert Colin McLean, George Tucker: Moral Philosopher and Man of Letters (Chapel Hill: University of North Carolina Press, 1961).

[5]"The Black Race," pp. 657-58.

[6]"The Black Race," p. 658.

[7]"The Black Race," p. 658.

[8]Philip Schaff, Slavery and the Bible (Chambersburg,

Pa.: M. Kieffer & Co., 1861), p. 7.

[9]Gayraud S. Wilmore, Black Religion and Black Radicalism (New York: Doubleday & Company, 1972), pp. 163-67. See also pp. 46-47, above.

[10]It was suggested in "The Black Race," quoted above. Frederick A. Ross, Slavery Ordained of God (1857; rpt. Miami: Mnemosyne Pub. Co., 1969) was the other.

[11]Ross, pp. 25, 30.

[12]Baldwin, pp. 455-57; see also African Servitude (New York: Davies & Kent, 1860), pp. 17-18.

[13]Thornton Stringfellow, Slavery (New York: J. F. Trow, 1861), pp. 12, 35.

[14]Baldwin, p. 444.

[15]Baldwin, pp. 173-75; and Samuel A. Cartwright, Essays ... Dooming Canaan to Be Servant of Servants (Vidalia, La.: n.p., 1843), pp. 9-10. Cartwright's Essays was revised from an earlier article: "Canaan Identified with the Ethiopian," Southern Quarterly Review 2 (Oct. 1842), 321-83.

[16]Baldwin, pp. 118-19.

[17]Stringfellow, p. 35.

[18]Baldwin, pp. 445-46.

[19]Cartwright, Essays, pp. 9-11.

[20]Baldwin, p. 17.

[21]See pp. 45-48, above.

[22]John Bachman, The Doctrine of the Unity of the Human Race (Charleston, S.C.: C. Canning, 1850), pp. 241-43.

[23]Robert Lewis Dabney, A Defense of Virginia (1867; rpt. New York: Negro Universities Press, 1969), p. 104.

[24]See the table on p. 103 and the map on p. 104.

The table obviously does not include the anonymous versions, which would expand the list of major exponents a bit more. Many other minor exponents, such as Thomas Cobb and Thomas Smyth, will be found throughout this study. I am including as major exponents those authors whose usage of the Ham myth seems central to one of their topics. Obviously, such a criterion is imprecise and even arbitrary. John England and Alexander McCaine almost did not make the "major" listing, and Thomas Smyth nearly did. But in my judgment England referred to the story of Ham *in order to make* his point, while Smyth referred to it *in order to salvage* his line of reasoning that had become contradictory.

I have emphasized those journals with widespread appeal in the antebellum South as a whole, rather than regional or parochial ones. I do not therefore claim to have found all the story-tellers.

I have not included bibliographic information in the table, since those who wish to can easily find the information in the bibliography and the various notes in each chapter.

[25] Josiah Clark Nott and George R. Gliddon, *Types of Mankind* (Philadelphia: Lippincott, Grambo, 1854), p. 496 and *passim*.

[26] See Clifford Geertz, *The Interpretation of Cultures* (New York: Basic Books, 1973), p. 114.

## Chapter VI

## THE MYTH OF HAM AMONG WHITE ANTEBELLUM SOUTHERNERS

The proponents of slavery in the antebellum South largely rejected two possible rationales for validating their peculiar institution. One violated their biblical world view and the other, their racial ethos. Previous chapters have suggested, first, that Southerners who understood their universe in biblical terms spurned polygenesis, since it contravened a literal interpretation of Genesis and the theological doctrines of original sin and redemption, and second, that Southerners who believed in the inherent inferiority of the black race generally balked at George Fitzhugh's opinion that slavery's justification should rest almost exclusively on social and economic theories, since the natural distinctions between whites and blacks would become blurred by establishing the principle of white slavery. The "middle ground" lay with those Christian racists who resisted demoting the black race to a less-than-human status and who, yet, maintained that a clear boundary separated the inherently inferior Negro from the Caucasian.

Southern Christians who appealed to the Ham myth were most apt to use it when they encountered the central paradox in the proslavery argument: if all people descended from Adam and Eve and were therefore brothers and sisters, then how could whites enslave blacks, especially black Christians? Thomas Smyth, a Presbyterian minister in Charleston, for example, turned to the curse of Ham when his reasoning became clearly contradictory. In attacking the polygenists, he asserted that black Christians had the same moral nature as white Christians. But this undermined the popular defense of slavery based on the racist assumption that the blacks were innately inferior to whites and would lead immoral lives when emancipated. Smyth, a firm defender of slavery, could not accept the logical conclusion of his reasoning--namely that blacks who were Christians should be emancipated. Although he had made little use of the Ham story in his overall argument, he nevertheless found the curse of Ham persuasive for resolving the central paradox on the grounds that all human suffering resulted from original sin. Ham's "original sin" caused his descendants to suffer under the yoke of slavery just as Eve's sin caused all women to suffer in childbirth and Adam's sin caused all humans to suffer from diseases and death.[1]

Smyth's argument, drawn from the story of Ham, seems unconvincing to people today because it is so alien to contemporary cultural ideas and values. But the story of Noah and his three sons functioned as myth in the antebellum South, as previous chapters have argued, becuase it symbolically brought together the whites' racial stereotypes, political theories, religious beliefs, and economic realities. How did the structure of the Ham story help resolve tensions in the white Southerners' world? How did the story function as a religious symbol system in the white Southern culture?

## World View, Ethos, and Religious Symbols

Studying a culture is like studying a river system with the general contour dug in its surrounding countryside, with the geological formations that impede and change its course, and with the general force of its current. One cannot really understand the current by simply studying the whirlpools and velocity without accounting for the general contour and geological formations; nor the general contour without looking at the rock formations and the force and volume of water; nor the geological obstacles that affect the river's course without understanding the current and the general outline of the river system.

Similarly the white Southerners' dominant world view, their racial ethos, and the Ham myth in the antebellum South are interrelated. Their biblical view of the universe is understandable only in terms of the symbols that made it persuasive and the racial values and institutions that influenced its character. Their attitudes about slavery make more sense within the context of their world view and the symbol systems that gave daily life meaning. The Ham myth is primarily significant as a symbol system that synthesized their dominant world view and their racial ethos.

World view, according to Clifford Geertz, encompasses a people's "most comprehensive ideas of order." It is "their picture of the way things in sheer actuality are, their concept of nature, of self, of society."[2] World view is an elusive category for three reasons. First, a people's overall conception of the universe and their place in it is almost always implicit. Their most fundamental idea of reality cannot really become explicit until it is challenged by an alternative system, and then its assumed validity is undermined. Whenever a world view loses its sense of "givenness," then it is no longer persuasive, or is at least less persuasive. Second, a people's view of the universe continually adapts to new knowledge and fluctuating beliefs. In modern societies, changes in economic systems, in ethical values, and in science and technology occur rapidly--sometimes so rapidly that a people's world view gets shattered. Third, a world view comprises a total system of thought and therefore cannot be divided into parts. Yet, an analysis of a people's most fundamental ideas of order involves dividing their universe into conceptual categories, thus endangering the apprehension of world view as totality.

It is especially difficult to describe world view in the antebellum South because of competing visions among Southerners of their universe, themselves, and their civilization. Between 1831 and 1861 there were at least three different groundings for the Southern world view: the Enlightenment rationalism of the founding fathers, the scientific theory of the American School of Ethnology, and the biblical interpretation of America as the New Israel. The abolitionists, who had interpreted the revolutionary leaders' theories of government to suit their own purposes, were partially responsible for the Southerners' turning away from Enlightenment rationalism to a biblical view of human nature and social progress. At almost the same time, the polygenetic theories of some ethnologists and the concomitant beliefs that blacks were less than human challenged a world view based on a literal interpretation of the Bible. And many more perspectives arose as individuals attempted to understand their universe by finding new grounds without necessarily discarding old ones. At times Locke's theory of human rights and duties became joined to the biblical doctrine of original sin. At other times popularizers of the new ethnological research tried, without much success, to fit their theories with the biblical account of creation. To make matters more difficult, the open debate about the nature of the universe led Southerners to question the aura of factuality that normally supports a world view.

In the thirty-year period before the Civil War a certain interpretation of the Bible as the constitution for the advance of Southern civilization became the dominant grounding for the Southerners' world view. "Dominant" does not mean that all Southerners based their view of the universe on the Bible--there were those who preferred to adapt the revolutionary leaders' concepts to fit the almost universally accepted belief among white Southerners in the 1830's that black bondage in America was there to stay; there were others who tried to explain human nature and social order by polygenetic theories that established the intellectual and moral superiority of the white race. Nor does dominance mean that the white Southerners' belief system was so stable that they could disregard challenges from the opponents of slavery in the North and from segments of their own society. Dominance does mean, however, that the Bible provided the most acceptable basis for the Southerners' "universe," one adopted by large segments of the society for establishing fundamental order in the world, in terms of which their institutions, customs, and values could be meaningfully understood.

The biblical world view in the antebellum South neatly circumscribed both the white Southerners' views about social order and their understanding of American destiny in the world. The doctrine of original sin explained both the inevitability of human suffering and the need for governmental institutions to check people's sinful predispositions. Southerners did not, therefore, gravitate toward utopian solutions to human suffering. They rather hoped to build and preserve institutions where enlightened self-interest would coincide with humane governmental control. The institution of the family provided the best model for social control since its authority structure was based on natural distinctions among people, and yet enlightened self-interest kept power from being abused. Indeed, in patriarchal times God had ordained familial relationships to minimize the chaos and suffering that resulted from Adam's and Eve's original sin. Southern Christians, who had renewed the Puritan vision that America was the New Israel, could easily identify themselves with the ancient patriarchs. Since God had, after all, blessed the patriarchal form of government in the days of Noah and Abraham, it seemed likely that he would also bless America if her citizens tried to build their civilization according to the biblical laws established by God in the Old Testament. Thus, although Southern Christians felt that they could not build utopian institutions, they saw the hand of divine providence blessing American civilization. If they conformed to God's law revealed in the Bible, God would help them build a great civilization that would spiritually enlighten the rest of the world.

The Southerners' biblical world view did not, however, develop in a vacuum. The economic realities of the slave-labor system, the social attitudes formed by life on the plantations, the racial stereotypes patterned by the whites' relationship with blacks all helped shape the actual values in the Southerners' daily lives. Geertz calls the valuational part of human experience "ethos": "A people's ethos is the tone, character, and quality of their life, its moral and aesthetic style and mood; it is the underlying attitude toward themselves and their world that life reflects."[3] Of course racial values in the antebellum South varied considerably among different strata of society and even from family to family. The various groundings of world view in the antebellum South provide one way to classify the racial ethos. For example, the racism of ethnologists who understood the universe in terms of science was generally more virulent than that of Christians who based their world view on biblical stories. Likewise, Southerners who saw the universe in terms of Enlightenment rationalism differed subtly in their ethical appraisals of slavery from those who accepted a biblical interpretation. This study focuses on the racial ethos of white Christians.

Slavery was an ethical institution, the Christian racists argued, because the relationship between master and slave provided the most equitable arrangement possible between two races of people with inherently different mental abilities and moral predispositions. These advocates of slavery never denied that the planters gained profits from their slaves' labor; they did, however, insist that the Southern system of labor maximized the slaves' well-being when compared to the exploited capitalist workers in the Northern states and in England. They never denied that a few Simon Legrees had on rare occasion besmirched their peculiar institution; they were convinced, however, that they could reform slavery if Northern abolitionists would stop inciting their slaves to revolt. In any case, they contended, patriarchal servitude best served the interests of blacks and of Southern society. The peculiar institution both controlled the Africans' predisposition to lascivious and socially disruptive behavior and exposed them to Christianity.

The Southern world view and ethos were closely intertwined, mutually confirming and supporting one another. The everyday values of the society, codified in customs and laws, encouraged by racial attitudes, and enforced by social institutions became intellectually and emotionally persuasive when they fit neatly into the Southerners' picture of the universe. For example, the conservative theory of government for managing the less educated and weaker members of society legitimized the control of blacks. In turn, the Southern ethos became the experiential evidence to support the society's fundamental ideas about universal order. The Southerners' socially constructed world with its customs, attitudes, and institutions validated their understanding of the universe. The racial ethos, for example, tended to authenticate the biblical world view since white attitudes about the inferiority of blacks reinforced belief in humanity's "fallen" state.

A widely circulated essay by William Gilmore Simms on the morality of slavery illustrates how well the Southerners' racial ethos fit with their biblical world view. In concluding his essay, Simms argued that Christianizing Southern slaves had elevated their intellects and morals. Blacks, however, had "no capacity for an individual independent existence, but ... were always designed for a subordinate one." In general, God had created the black race to be "an implement in the hands of civilization always," and blacks were morally and intellectually unsuited for liberty and social equality; in particular, Negro slavery in the South was especially fortuitous since blacks labored well in a tropical climate and their Christian masters guarded their moral development and provided them with adequate food, clothing, and shelter. In America the "original genius" of the "Anglo-Americans" had been strengthened through their struggle in a hostile environment, producing an "individuality of character" among those who were creating a new social order. Simms believed that black slavery, "as the destined agent for ... civilization," would expand beyond the Southern states into Mexico and Latin America.[4]

Thus, in abbreviated form Simms joined the major elements of the racial ethos with the dominant world view in the antebellum South: blacks were innately inferior to whites; Southern masters governed blacks justly and temperately; slavery humanely controlled blacks, protecting their own best interests and those of society; God ordained Negro servitude in America in order to help whites who were building a new social order. While Simms' essay exhibits an overall congruence between the Southerners' world view and their racial ethos, vacillation and hedging at certain points reveal some strain. A basic tension in the proslavery argument of moderate racists involves the extent to which blacks were considered fully human. Unlike polygenists, Christians in the antebellum South did not relegate blacks to a subhuman status in theory, though they did insist on subordinating blacks to whites in practice. The table on page 116 schematizes the various dimensions of this basic contradiction.

While Simms' essay displays, or at least implies, all dimensions of this basic contradiction, it is most evident in the ethical and political spheres. Insisting that blacks had made tremendous intellectual and moral progress in America under the tutelage of white Christians, he speculated that blacks might in the distant future "rise, morally and intellectually," to the level of whites and thereby deserve emancipation: "It is possible that a time will come, when, taught by our schools and made strong by our training, the negroes of the Southern States may arrive at freedom; then, at least, his condition may be such as would entitle him to go forth out of bondage." Yet in the very same paragraph he undercut this vague, future hope by declaring that the historical evidence of the blacks' inferiority "ought to be conclusive, with every person of common sense, not only that they have no capacity for an individual independent existence, but that they were always designed for a subordinate one."[5]

In arguing against a literal interpretation of the doctrine that all men were created equal, Simms contended that the new political order in America did not support an absolute social equality among all people, but rather upheld each individual's right "to rise honorably above his fellows." According to Simms, the founding fathers really asserted that "each man should enjoy the place to which he is justly entitled, by reason of his moral [character], his intellect, his strength, or his resource." Yet in defending slavery, Simms treated blacks as an "inferior class"; individual Negroes did not have the right to liberty until they became "a successful people."[6]

Previous chapters have already presented examples of the conflicting views of moderate racists in the theological, economic, and social spheres. Theologically, Christian racists believed that blacks and whites descended from the same original parents and were therefore brothers and sisters. They argued that the polygenetic hypothesis was heretical

| Dimensions | Polarities and Tensions in the Proslavery Argument of Moderate Racists | |
|---|---|---|
| Theological | Through Christ, all persons--blacks and whites--have possibility of redemption. | Blacks are not to be treated as brothers and sisters. |
| Ethical | Through Christian training blacks are progressing in morality. | Inherent intellectual (and perhaps moral) inferiority precludes blacks' developing the same moral sensitivity as whites. |
| Political | The new social order in America involves each individual's right to self-determination. | Blacks as a race have no rights to self-determination and must always be enslaved. |
| Economic | Blacks as workers are invaluable to Southern economy. | Blacks are inherently lazy and irresponsible. |
| Social | Blacks are trustworthy and loyal. | Blacks' inherent tendency to immorality and violence presents a threat to society. |

because Christ suffered and died for all humanity; the doctrines of atonement and redemption presupposed that Adam's and Eve's original sin affected blacks and whites alike. Yet the advocates of slavery argued that blacks should be enslaved because they were inherently inferior to whites. Even when individual blacks became Christians, they, as members of a subordinate race, were not to be treated as equals. Economically, the same Southerners who argued that the black, slave-labor force was indispensable to the Southern economy frequently portrayed the Negro as inherently lazy. Socially, those who claimed that blacks were entirely trustworthy and loyal to their masters often defended harsh laws to control slaves out of fear that the Negroes' volatile nature and physical strength might lead to insurrection, especially if abolitionists infiltrated their ranks.

Religious symbols have traditionally functioned to overcome such social tensions by synthesizing a people's ethos with their world view. The Ham story functioned as myth in the antebellum South because it symbolically framed the ethos of plantation life within a sacred history. The Ham myth, as a sacred story, provided a context for legitimizing the whites' racial attitudes and slavery in terms of divine purpose.

## The Structure of the Ham Myth

Claude Lévi-Strauss's theory of myth holds that structural polarities within a myth mediate oppositions and contradictions in people's thoughts and in their society. Lévi-Strauss writes that myths "provide a logical model capable of overcoming a contradiction."[7] His theory is particularly useful in showing how polarities in the Ham myth paralleled the cultural tensions in white attitudes, beliefs, and actions in the antebellum South. Lévi-Strauss believes, however, that the narrative quality of a myth is unimportant except as an artificial device to hold the polarities together. For the Southern versions of the Ham myth, however, the narrative mode of expression is not a secondary characteristic since the dramatic series of events themselves provide the mythic resolution of the conflicts.[8] Attention to the narrative events in the Ham story that resolved the structural polarities in the myth and their corresponding cultural tensions enhances rather than undercuts Lévi-Strauss's theory. For the dramatic events that mediate both the oppositions in the myth and the contradictions in the proslavery argument also forge a synthesis between the Southerners' biblical world view and their racial ethos. Consequently Lévi-Strauss's structural perspective becomes joined to Clifford Geertz's cultural model; a detailed analysis of the Ham myth's structure then augments the historical method of exploring a people's world view and ethos. The table on p. 118 schematizes the oppositions in the Ham myth, shows the corresponding contradictions in white attitudes, beliefs, and actions, and relates the mythic event which mediated the contradictions and oppositions by forging a synthesis between an element of the white racial ethos and a particular belief drawn from the Southerners' world view.

From the structuralist perspective there are five basic oppositions in the Ham myth: (A-I) Only one family survives the flood, but Noah fathers three sons of different colors and temperaments; (B-I) Noah is righteous and his family is saved, but Ham commits an indecent, sexual act and is

STRUCTURAL TABLE

| | I OPPOSITIONS IN MYTH | | II CONTRADICTIONS IN WHITE ATTITUDES, BELIEFS, AND ACTIONS | | III MEDIATION IN MYTH | IV MYTHIC UNIFICATION OF | |
|---|---|---|---|---|---|---|---|
| | | | | | | WORLD VIEW | ETHOS |
| A | Only *one* family survives the flood. | Noah fathers *three* sons of different colors and temperaments. | Through conversion to Christianity all men of every race are equally saved. | Blacks are not treated as brothers. | A new creation of races in the family of Noah: Japheth--white; Shem--red; Ham--black. | All men are descended from Adam (human unity). | Blacks are inferior species (racial diversity). |
| B | Noah is righteous and his family is saved. | Ham commits an indecent sexual act and is condemned. | Blacks have made great moral progress in the South. | Blacks are enslaved because of inherent tendency to immorality. | Noah blessed Japheth & Shem because of good deeds; cursed Ham because of sinfulness. | Suffering is the result of Original Sin. | Slavery, which controls black immorality, is a moral institution. |
| C | Ham acted like a foolish child (laughing and joking about his father). | Ham acted like a villain (the heinous sexual crime). | Blacks are trustworthy and loyal to their masters. | Blacks have inherent tendency to immorality and violence. | Prophetic Decree: Ham is to be his brothers' slave. | God's laws promote social harmony. | Slavery is moral because it is a patriarchal institution. |
| D | Japheth and Shem earn Noah's blessings. | Ham merits Noah's curse. | The new social order in America involves each individual's right to self-determination. | Blacks have no rights to self-determination. | Ham, Shem, and Japheth encounter each other in America in fulfillment of prophetic decree. | America is the stage for the final scene in the divine plan for human destiny. | Slavery is a social and economic necessity. |
| E | Ham helps Japheth build a great civilization by doing menial tasks. | Ham is not to amalgamate with his brothers nor participate fully in the new social order. | Blacks are invaluable to the southern economy. | Blacks do not share whites' attitudes about the value of labor, and are lazy. | Prophetic Decree: Japheth shall be enlarged, dwell in Shem's tents, and enslave Ham. | America is the new Israel, founded on biblical principles. | Blacks must be forced to work; their insouciant character precludes equality. |

condemned; (C-I) Ham acted like a foolish child, yet he acted like a villain; (D-I) Japheth and Shem earn Noah's blessings, but Ham merits Noah's curse; (E-I) Ham helps Japheth build a great civilization by doing menial tasks, but Ham is not to amalgamate with his brothers nor participate fully in the new social order. Since myth mediates contradictions in society these five structural oppositions correspond with polarities in the white culture of the antebellum South.

First, the polarity of only one family's surviving the flood vs. Noah's fathering three sons of different colors and temperaments (A-I) parallels the Southern desire to Christianize blacks without allowing them to participate in American society as equals (A-II). The proponents of slavery argued that the sons of Ham were gaining a great blessing in learning the truths of the gospel under the beneficent tutelage of the sons of Japheth. Yet they argued that blacks were inferior to whites and could never be treated as brothers. The Ham myth mediates this tension by describing the origin of the three distinct races in the family of Noah (A-III). Thus, the fundamental belief that all men are descended from Adam becomes congruent with white attitudes about black inferiority (A-IV). For some purposes, then, the human family was one, yet for other purposes races were diverse.

Second, the polarity of righteous Noah who is saved vs. sinful Ham who is condemned (B-I) corresponds to the contradictory claims that blacks in the South had made great moral progress yet slavery is justifiable on the grounds that blacks were inherently immoral (B-II). The Christian racists in the South believed that slavery was a moral institution because it controlled the sinful predispositions of the black race. Yet they insisted that Christianity raised blacks to a high moral level. White clergymen usually maintained that there were no differences in the moral nature of the two races. The claim that an entire race should be controlled by slavery ignored the moral level attained by individual black Christians. Noah's blessing of Japheth and Shem because they were righteous while cursing Ham because he was sinful mediates this contradiction (B-III). Whites who held the biblical world view believed that human suffering was the result of an original sin; therefore, Noah's curse on Ham forged a congruence between the belief that suffering was caused by sin and black bondage in America (B-IV). Just as death and the pains of childbirth were the results of Adam's and Eve's disobedience, slavery was the result of Ham's sexual crime.

Third, the opposition of Ham, the villain, who commits a serious crime, and Ham, the foolish child, who does not understand the seriousness of his act (C-I) parallels a basic paradox in the whites' attitudes toward the black race. Southerners argued two seemingly contradictory points of view: the South had nothing to fear because its slaves were entirely loyal to their masters, yet the large numbers of blacks in the South created a dangerous situation and the society could easily be destroyed by racial war (C-II). The prophetic decree that Ham should be his brothers' slave (C-III) mediates the two halves of the paradox by unifying the Southern belief that God's laws promote social harmony with the justification of slavery as a patriarchal institution (C-IV). Exponents of the Ham myth argued that if Northerners would only understand that Noah's curse was authorized by God to promote good social order by controlling the blacks' sinful tendencies (their sensuality, lasciviousness, and warlike nature), the deep divisions between North and South could be healed. Like children, blacks needed firm authority. They should be controlled by slavery without being abused. Whites who understood the nature and temperament of blacks by treating them firmly without tyranny wisely administered God's law, thereby controlling the blacks' sinful predispositions and maintaining social harmony.

Fourth, the polarity of Japheth's and Shem's earning Noah's blessings while Ham merited his curse (D-I) parallels the contradiction of excluding a whole race from the American political vision that each individual may advance to the highest position that accords with his physical and mental abilities and his moral character (D-II). Southerners believed that they were preserving the noble experiment of the new nation founded on the principles of liberty. George Fitzhugh wrote that "No man loves liberty and hates slavery so cordially as the Southerner. Liberty is with him a privilege, or distinction, belonging to all white men."[9] Northern abolitionists pointed out the inconsistency of Southerners' picturing themselves as the conservers of the national heritage while they held men and women as slaves. Depicting Ham's, Shem's, and Japheth's encounter in America as the fulfillment of a divine decree, the myth attempted to mediate the political contradiction by showing that each race's destiny was predetermined by God (D-III). Thus, the myth incorporated the whites' justification of slavery as a social and economic necessity within the Southerners' belief that America was the stage for the final scene in the divine plan for human destiny (D-IV).

Finally, the polarity of Ham's serving Japheth to build a great civilization without participating in the fruits of his labor (E-I) corresponds to another paradox in white attitudes toward the black race. On the one hand, blacks were good workers who were invaluable to the Southern economy; on the other hand, they were lazy by nature (E-II). While the slaves were indispensable for the advance of Southern civilization, they could not be assimilated into it. Southerners believed that they were creating a New Israel based on biblical principles; to build the new nation slave labor was necessary, yet the slaves could never share in the great achievement (E-IV). The prophetic decree unified the world view and ethos while mediating the economic contradiction by assigning definite roles to the three races for advancing human civilization (E-III).

NOTES

[1]Thomas Smyth, _The Unity of the Human Races_ (1851), _Complete Works of Rev. Thomas Smyth, D.D._, ed. J. Wm. Flinn, 10 vols. (Columbia, S.C.: R. L. Bryan, 1910), VIII, 110, 128, 312-14, and _passim_.

[2]Clifford Geertz, _The Interpretation of Cultures_ (New York: Basic Books, 1973), p. 127; see also p. 89. I am drawing heavily on Geertz's anthropological theory in this section to help interpret the symbolic function of the Ham myth among white Southerners in the antebellum period.

[3]Geertz, p. 127; see also p. 89.

[4]William Gilmore Simms, "The Morals of Slavery," _The Pro-Slavery Argument_ (1852; rpt. New York: Negro Universities Press, 1968), pp. 270-74.

[5]Simms, pp. 269-70.

[6]Simms, pp. 257-68.

[7]Claude Lévi-Strauss, _Structural Anthropology_ (1958; New York: Basic Books, 1963), pp. 229-30 and _passim_.

[8]Percy S. Cohen insists that narration is an important part of all myths and is not a secondary characteristic. See his critique of Lévi-Strauss in "Theories of Myth," _Man; The_

Journal of the Royal Anthropological Institute 4 (Sept. 1969), 347-48.

[9]George Fitzhugh, "Southern Thought," De Bow's Review 23 (Oct. 1857), 349.

## Chapter VII

## THE HAM MYTH AS SYMBOL SYSTEM

In most general terms, a myth is a complex of religious symbols composed as a story. The Ham story functioned as myth in the antebellum South because the individual episodes synthesized the white Southerners' racial ethos with their biblical world view and thereby resolved social tensions that arose because white Christians held blacks in bondage. The most casual reader, no doubt, has noticed that the mythic expressions quoted in previous chapters are unlike ordinary discursive language. Mythic thought, indeed, does differ from historical and scientific thinking. What is the particular symbolic expression of mythic language? Why are myths so persuasive in a culture? Can stories really become persuasive, authoritative myths in modern, pluralistic societies?

### The Nature of Myth

I define myth as a narrative irreducible to fact or fiction, whose language conveys the passive voice, the imperative mood, and the continuous progressive tense.[1] This definition is drawn from an analysis of American versions of the myth of Noah and his three sons. It therefore characterizes the expressions of the Ham story in the antebellum South. Examples from the Priest version of the Ham myth will illustrate, first, the significance of grammatic style.

First, mythic language conveys the passive voice:

> GOD ... superintended the formation of two of the sons of NOAH, in the womb of their mother, in an extraordinary and supernatural manner, giving to these two children such forms of bodies, constitutions of natures, and complexions of skin, as suited his will. Those two sons were JAPHETH and HAM. Japheth He caused to be born white ... while He caused Ham to be born black.[2]

Myths persuade by appealing to an order of existence beyond human control. Even when the principal human characters in a mythic drama appear to be the agents of an action, they either act in accordance with certain universal laws and are rewarded, or act against them and are punished. Thus, for example, Oedipus transgresses the incest taboos and is blinded, or Adam and Eve eat the fruit and are excluded from the garden. The passive voice of mythic language expresses the "givenness" of creation and thus sets the boundaries for human action. In this way myths uphold the social order by blocking off rational explanations and alternative ways of acting.

The Ham myth supported subordination of the black race so authoritatively because Ham and Japheth are presented as puppets whose strings are pulled by God. In the anonymous text from the <u>Southern Literary Messenger</u> (pp. 93-94, above) neither Ham nor Japheth are independent actors: "something whispers" them both that they have a mission to perform, only fully known to God; Ham is sent to America "by the Great Being who rules and guides us all" in order to help with the menial tasks of building a new spiritual civilization; Ham does not consider Japheth responsible for his enslavement, but rather believes that slavery is part of divine destiny. In the Cartwright version (pp. 99-100, above) the language similarly conveys the passive voice. Ham, Shem, and Japheth are agents of the action--"the prophecy ... was carried out"; Japheth "became enlarged, as had been foretold"; Ham "appeared on the beach ... as if drawn thither by an impulse of nature to fulfil his destiny"; Japheth "was compelled against his will" to enslave Ham rather than Shem, thereby carrying out "God's decree without knowing it."

Second, mythic language suggests the <u>imperative mood</u>:

> ... as God did make the two complexions of black and white originally, which characterize two races of men, that it is, therefore, no less a sin than <u>sacrilege</u> to amalgamate them, thereby destroying God's work, and supplying the ruin with adulterations.... [W]hites and blacks should not mingle races, and thereby <u>sin</u> against God in the mutilation of the original order.[3]

Myths either issue or imply enduring commands. They not only describe the origin of a particular institution, race, or pattern of human behavior, but also prescribe a people's actions and their social values. For example, Adam's fall not only explains the origin of human suffering, but also demands human obedience to God's laws. The Oedipus myth reinforces the incest taboo. Even when myths are not so explicitly injunctive as the quotation from the Ham myth above, there is by definition an underlying, if implicit, universal command.

By divine command Ham was enslaved to Japheth, and their sons were to avoid social and physical intercourse. Thus, the imperative mood conveyed God's laws for regulating the relationship between blacks and whites in America and consequently legitimized slavery and black subordination in the antebellum South as divine ordinances. According to the Baldwin version (p. 98, above) God "bade" Japheth "inherit and enter, possess and improve" the land of Shem; "He gave him the ancient commission to coerce the race of Ham to bear its part of tribute by tilling the soil and subduing the earth." In the anonymous version (pp. 93-94, above) Japheth insists that "our races are different," and he tells Ham that he "may participate" only in cutting the forest and reclaiming the soil; Ham responds by denying that he and his children are "worthy" of being admitted to Japheth's "higher sphere." Thus, the myth reinforced the social relationship between the two races in the South.

Third, mythic language suggests the <u>continuous progressive tense</u>:

> Noah's feeling on that occasion when he cursed Ham ... would be as follows: 'Oh Ham, my son, it is not for this <u>one deed</u> alone which you have just committed that I have, by God's command, thus condemned you and your race, but the Lord has shown me that all your descendants will, more or less, be like <u>you</u> their father, on which account, it is determined by the Creator that you and your people are to occupy the lowest condition of all the families among mankind, and even be enslaved as brute beasts.'[4]

Myths express timelessness by universalizing the concrete human experience. They provide that what was true in the past is true today and will be true in the future. Even when myths seemingly take place in a supposedly historical period (as does the Ham myth, for example), the time is so far removed that it is not susceptible to historical investigation. The characters in the myth become idealized into archetypes, representing certain classes, races, or even humanity itself; the actions of these archetypal beings give universal significance to the cultural situation of those who are grasped by the myth. Lévi-Strauss writes, "a myth always refers to events alleged to have taken place long ago. But what gives the myth operational value is that the specific pattern described is timeless; it explains the present and the past as well as the future."[5]

In the Southern versions of the Ham myth Japheth, Shem, and Ham become archetypes respectively for the white, red, and black races in America. The character of each race is established for all time by the actions of its progenitor. According to the Baldwin version (p. 98, above) there is "a universal and permanent trinity of races." In the Cartwright text (pp. 99-100, above) Ham fulfills "his destiny of becoming Japheth's servant" by an "impulse of his nature"; he cannot rebel against slavery because "it is contrary to the first principle of his nature." Thus, the whites' experience of racial diversity in the antebellum South became universalized through the mythic expressions of the story of Noah and his three sons.

Fourth, myth is <u>narrative</u>. The expression of myths as stories is significant because myths portray archetypal patterns of human behavior. Mircea Eliade writes that myths narrate "a sacred history," and relate events "that took place in primordial Time, the fabled time of the 'beginning.'"[6] In some sense, the tragedies, comedies, and struggles of daily life become repetitions and variations of a primordial drama for those who are grasped by a particular myth. Myths address those human patterns in life that people see as sequentially ordered and causally connected. For example, Christian mythology can explain the rise and fall of a corrupt political leader as a repetition of Adam's and Eve's pride, disobedience, and subsequent banishment; or the assassination of a statesman who had championed the rights of the poor as a variation of Christ's ministry and sacrifice on the cross for humanity.

Percy Cohen implicitly agrees with Eliade that myth is a narrative of sacred history that refers back to the beginning of time. Cohen, disagreeing with Lévi-Strauss, tries to show that the narrative quality of myth is essential since "narrative is an ordering of specific events." The ordering of events in a chronological sequence is important because "a narrative has a beginning, a moment of time in which a series of events is anchored." He argues that myth "anchors the present in the past." Thus, a "myth, by establishing a narrative, locks a set of circumstances" of the present "in an original set of events." Myth, he contends, is more important among traditional and conservative peoples, who are especially interested in legitimizing "existing social practices." He further suggests that "prophecy is a sort of myth in reverse" and emerges in societies where traditions are in the process of breaking down.[7]

Cohen's insight applies to American society prior to the Civil War. The South had retrenched into a conservative posture and was being forced by Northern abolitionists to defend its customs, beliefs, and institutions. Here, then, is one reason why the Ham myth had such power in the Southern consciousness. The demise of popularly-held institutions and beliefs, along with the pluralism in the North in the same period, may have accounted, at least partially, for the emergence of many new prophetic religions--e.g., such "dangerous 'isms,'" as Millerism and Mormonism that Southerners vigorously decried.

In any case, the Ham myth in the South did anchor the whites' racial ethos and their peculiar institution in a primordial past. The series of events in the myth--already described at length in terms of the creation of three distinct races in the family of Noah, Ham's heinous sin and Japheth's and Shem's filial respect, Noah's blessings and curse, Ham's degeneration into barbarism and idolatry, Shem's rejection of Christianity, Japheth's acceptance of Christianity, and God's unveiling America to become the spiritual center of the world--all formed a sacred story that allowed those grasped by it to make sense out of their experience. The blacks' supposed lack of morality and their enslavement became locked into the mythic framework of Ham's sin and Noah's curse. The difficulty of proselytizing among the Indians became grounded in Shem's rejection of Christianity. The whites' intellectual and moral achievements found an anchor in the mythic account of Japheth's respect for his father and Noah's blessing.

Fifth, myth is irreducible to fiction. Until recently, "myth" in popular usage generally denoted an unreal, false story or idea.[8] One still hears such statements as "it is only a myth that women are inferior to men." Anthropologists and historians of religions, however, have usually considered myths to be expressions of truth. In the vernacular "myth" is recovering its denotation as a distinct, and by no means exclusively ancient or primitive, way to express truth. For example, in a recent article in a popular newspaper a journalist discussed Diego Rivera's portrait of Hernando Cortés "as a hunchbacked, chinless man with sickly, gray skin, bulging eyes, a stubbled beard, a sharp nose, deformed, swollen knees and the general look of a cretin." Concluding a discussion of the mural, the journalist wrote, "But, whatever the lack of historical accuracy in the mural of Rivera, there is no doubt his portrait has mythological truth. Many Mexicans would like to think Cortés looked just the way Rivera painted him."[9]

When myths are taken as such, they convey and contain their own verity. For example, Rivera's portrait has mythological truth because it reveals contemporary Mexican values. Or, creation myths are true because they express people's attitudes about the world and about the worth of human life.[10] Thus, myths differ from artistic expressions because myths do not disengage "from the whole question of factuality," to quote Geertz. Art, on the other hand, may deliberately manufacture "an air of semblance and illusion." The artist is free to create his own world without slavishly representing reality. Myths are successful insofar as they "create an aura of utter actuality."[11] Myths are what they are insofar as people are convinced that their truths do, in fact, correspond to the real world.

How far can an historical study evaluate precisely the degree to which a particular story created "an aura of utter actuality" in a culture? The argument here that the story of Noah's three sons became a myth in the antebellum South is three-fold. First, the events and actors in the story accurately depicted and synthesized the Southerners' fundamental beliefs and racial values. Second, Ham's identification with the black race was widespread in the antebellum South and became part of the cultural vocabulary. Third, the major expositors of the story were prominent men in their communities who with only a couple of possible exceptions could hardly be classified as "crack-pots." These men presented the story of Noah's three sons in all seriousness. Others of like stature earnestly referred to the story of Ham to explain and justify blacks' subordination to whites in America.

The polemical character of the whole proslavery

argument does, however, raise questions about how firmly the Southerners held the story as factual. Black slavery existed; the story provided an explanation of how it began de divino. When a story is consciously used as causal explanation and taken as such, its factuality in the recipients' consciousness is at least seriously jeopardized. The story as causal polemic is, in the final analysis, inseparable from the story as myth. Psychohistorical proofs about each of the major exponents and of a wide selection of those who referred to the story of Ham are simply infeasible. Nevertheless, some evidence suggests that Southerners identified Ham as the progenitor of the black race apart from justifying slavery. On the other hand, James D. B. De Bow probably was not taken by the story as myth when he wrote that "immediately after the deluge, we have a decree of God, himself, condemning the children of Ham to perpetual servitude, using the very Hebrew word which translators render slave"; one month later he championed polygenesis to support black subordination.[12] But few are the examples which clearly fall into one or the other of these extremes. Propaganda may well be the way certain writers and certain readers used the Ham story in the antebellum South. But since the story brought coherence between world view and ethos, its clear expression in mythic language and its widespread usage in the antebellum South are sufficient reasons to regard the story as myth in its total impact on Southern society.

Nor were most versions of the Ham story in the antebellum South explicitly allegorical. Allegory is an artistic expression that at times approaches the symbolic persuasiveness of myth. For example, John Bunyan's Pilgrim's Progress treats such Christian themes as humility, faith, and doubt. Artistic manipulation of these themes might revitalize basic religious symbols for readers of the allegory who are already steeped in Christian symbolism. The character Christian's pilgrimage persuades insofar as readers make connections between the narrative line of the allegory and reality as expressed in their religious myths and rituals. Those who are influenced by the Christian world view may consciously accept all or part of Bunyan's interpretation of truth, or even deny it, and still retain their world view and their ethos intact. On the other hand, since the story of Christ's death and resurrection directly expresses a Christian truth, to reject it would necessarily mean adjusting or even abandoning their fundamental beliefs and values. Unlike allegory, there is no distinction in myth between the narrative line of the story and reality. The process of demythologization involves rewriting myths so that the religious symbols mediate other fundamental truths rather than express immediate truths. The symbolic persuasiveness of religious allegories, like that of religious paintings, novels, and other forms of artistic expression, depends largely on the degree to which they accurately represent or translate other more basic cultural truths.

The versions of the Ham myth quoted in this study directly depicted the relationship between the archetypal figures of Ham, Shem, and Japheth. For example, in the Cartwright text (pp. 99-100, above) Japheth was "cooped up in Europe," Japheth "unexpectedly discovered an unknown hemisphere," Japheth "became enlarged" and "literally dwelt in the tents of Shem," etc. One writer, however, constructed an explicit religious allegory based on the more basic myth. In the first part of Stringfellow's essay on slavery, the story of Ham is presented directly--that is, there is no distinction between the story line and reality. Stringfellow introduces the story through the literary device of having a son of Japheth approach an intelligent son of Ham in Africa to offer him the opportunity of becoming a slave. When the young African reflects on his condition, he ponders the history of his race:

> 'the Being who made this world, once destroyed by a flood of water all its inhabitants for their wickedness, except one man named Noah, and his three sons, Shem, Ham, and Japheth, and their wives. Ham, my father, was a compound of beastly wickedness.... The descendants of Japheth were distinguished for a progressive intelligence, and a commanding influence upon the destinies of the world....
>
> The descendants of Ham, the beastly and degraded son of Noah, were subjected to a degraded servitude to Shem and Japheth.[13]

In this passage blacks are identified as "descendants" of Ham, but there is no suggestion that the identification is in any way analogical or allegorical. Rather, the young African represents himself as the son of Ham in a literal sense.

Later in the same essay the story of Ham becomes analogical:

> Noah had three sons, Shem, Ham, and Japheth. These three sons are declared by the Almighty to be types of the several nations that would descend

> from them. They are made typical representatives of superior, inferior, and medium nations. Their several localities were selected of God for each class of these nations to occupy on the globe, and their habitations were adapted to their type of character.[14]

This passage introduces another section relating the story of Ham, Shem, and Japheth to the American experience. Although the subsequent story again reverts to mythic language, rather than analogical, the reader nevertheless is primed to regard the story as allegorical. This does not mean, however, that the story loses its mythic force; it does mean that its mythic force depends on readers' consciously making the connection between the narrative and reality.

Sixth, while myths directly express cultural truths, mythic truth is _not reducible to scientific facts or historical events_. Scientists who believe that a particular hypothesis does not explain physical phenomena exhaustively will accept, modify, or abandon current theories depending on carefully conducted experiments. Likewise, historians who recognize that their reconstructions of the past are interpretations will remain open to new interpretations of historical events. Mythological propositions, however, do not yield to scientific and historical analysis because their basis in reality includes a subjective and emotional involvement with the world. Myths are supported by a people's collective hopes and fears, by their attitudes and institutions, and by their beliefs about universal order. While scientific and historical studies may prove myths factually false, myths remain true, in the sense that they verify a people's shared feelings, social values, and commonly held beliefs. Elizabeth Janeway writes,

> Facts can be disproved, and theories based on them will yield in time to rational arguments and proof that they don't work. But myth has its own, furious, inherent reason-to-be because it is tied to desire. Prove it false a hundred times, and it will still endure because it is true as an expression of feeling.[15]

Mythological "truth," however, is not based solely on people's psychological hopes and fears. Unlike neuroses, myths are communal; they are shared meaning systems, based on real social values and beliefs. Neuroses refer to individuals' particular fantasies, unsupported by social reality.[16]

Myths, functioning as religious symbols, maintain a people's socially constructed world; they unify a culture by becoming acceptable symbol systems to affirm a people's social values and beliefs. As long as they continue to uphold a society's "plausibility structure," to borrow a term from Peter Berger, they are validated by the social reality, and are therefore "true." Mythological "truth," then, is relative and holds as long as the plausibility structure accords with a people's ethos and their world view.[17]

To call the story of Ham a myth, then, means that the narrative was at least more than a fanciful account, for it encompassed mythological truth insofar as it symbolized the white Southerners' experiences and beliefs. The Ham myth encapsulated the aspirations and fears of white Southerners in their relationship to blacks in the antebellum period. It was not symbolic fiction or explicit allegory (though at times Southerners allegorized the myth) because its narrative line directly portrayed and synthesized the Southerners' biblical world view and their racial ethos. Nor was its historic or scientific accuracy at issue for the Southerners who took it as a true account of the origins of Negro slavery. Through the myth's expression in language conveying the passive voice, the imperative mood, and the continuous progressive tense, it forcibly validated white beliefs about black inferiority, it legitimized Negro slavery as ordained by God, and it prescribed the proper relationship that should always exist between blacks and whites.

## Myth and Modernity

Myths are authoritative and persuasive in traditional cultures not only because they synthesize a people's world view and their ethos, but also because there are no alternatives; people do not have the option of choosing their myths, values, and beliefs. As long as there are no outside challenges to the system (such as the white man's arrival among the American Indians, for example), myths are taken for granted and successfully legitimize the values of daily life and reconfirm ideas about the nature of the universe. Modern societies, on the other hand, are pluralistic. Since people living in the antebellum South participated in both regional and national cultures, they were in the presence of many competing value and belief systems. To some degree at least, they could pick and choose their style of life and even the theories and ideas that came to express their world view.

Berger describes this shift from traditional to modern cultures:

> The key characteristic of all pluralistic situations ... is that the religious ex-monopolies can no longer take for granted the allegiance of their client populations. Allegiance is voluntary and thus, by definition, less than certain. As a result, the religious traditions, which previously could be authoritatively imposed, now has to be marketed. It must be 'sold' to a clientele that is no longer constrained to 'buy.'[18]

In modern societies, then, myths lack the authoritative persuasiveness they have in traditional societies. A particular myth cannot be the solution for synthesizing a people's ethos and their world view, but only a possible one. This study does not claim that the Ham story was myth for everyone in the antebellum South, but only that the story was widespread among those Southerners who believed that slavery could not be abolished and who also believed in Southern civilization as God's New Israel. The story became myth because it provided viable symbols for legitimizing the racial ethos in terms of a world view based on interpreting the Bible literally as the constitution for the South.

Myth in traditional societies has the explanatory function of describing the universe and the religious function of legitimizing values and beliefs by synthesizing a people's world view and their ethos. These two functions are inseparable: myth explains because it successfully forges congruence between a people's fundamental conception of the universe and their values; it legitimizes a culture's values and beliefs through religious symbols because it is taken as a true description of the universe. In modern societies, however, science has generally replaced myth in performing an explanatory function. Insofar as people in modern cultures tend to seek religious answers to validate their experiences and intuitions, myths are still relevant. According to Geertz, "The tendency to synthesize world view and ethos at some level, if not logically necessary, is at least empirically coercive; if it is not philosophically justified, it is at least pragmatically universal."[19]

The Ham myth in the antebellum South clearly served the religious function of legitimizing racial values and beliefs by symbolically forging a congruence between world view and ethos. Yet, since Southerners looked to science for explaining reality, the myth did not stand entirely on its own as a sacred story. Proponents of slavery argued for the myth's viability by buttressing it with scientific arguments. Thus, for example, they frequently joined mythic expressions of the Ham story to arguments adapted from science: philology was introduced to prove that ham meant "black" in ancient Hebrew; archeology, to show that the black race had not evolved since the time of Noah; ethnology and anatomy, to illustrate differences between the black and white races; history, to indicate the Africans' lack of civilization.

Science's "objective" persuasiveness and myth's "subjective" allure are incompatible. Myth tends to be undermined whenever logic and rationality are introduced, because its absolute "facticity can no longer be taken for granted."[20] And science that succumbs to assumptions and preconceptions loses its impartiality. Generally, scientific and historical arguments did not prevent the story of Noah and his three sons from functioning as myth because the story primarily persuaded on an experiential, intuitive level, rather than on a logical one. Scientific arguments often preserved the myth's viability by legitimizing its symbols as a true description of the universe in modern terminology. At times the myth bent science more than science undermined the myth; Samuel A. Cartwright, for example, not only selected factual data in order to authenticate the Genesis story, but even presented fanciful "evidence."[21]

At other times, however, science and history directly challenged the Ham myth as a factual account of racial origins. Ethnologists who comprised the American School proposed a polygenetic theory that the various races were independently created in diverse geographical regions. Historical inquiry led Robert L. Dabney, a prominent Presbyterian clergyman in Virginia, to reject Ham, Shem, and Japheth as archetypes of the black, red, and white races in America; he could not find incontrovertible evidence to prove that blacks were descendants of Ham.[22] Yet scientific theories and historical inquiries did not forge symbolic congruence between the dominant, biblical world view and the racial ethos in the South to furnish a religious solution to the Southerners' quest for meaning.

Exponents of the Ham myth argued that the account in Genesis 9 was true because it explained known facts about the character of the black, white, and red races, and because it accorded with God's will as revealed in the Bible for the American nation. Since the Southern story-tellers introduced rational argumentation, they often seemed to adopt the myth consciously, rather than being subconsciously embraced by it. Since Southerners introduced rationality into the mythic structure of the Ham story itself, the question again arises, this time on a more subtle and troubling level, whether the story was actually myth in the antebellum South at all. Eric Voegelin distinguishes "myth" as an expression of a people's primary experience of the universe from "mytho-speculation" which "holds an intermediate position between cosmological compactness and noetic differentiation." People in stable cultures are grasped by myths precisely because they accept them "without further questions." When questions arise about the "adequacy" of a particular myth for explaining physical phenomena or social values "it is no longer quite the process that has resulted in the myth of unquestioned acceptance. The process cannot be raised into consciousness without injecting questioning consciousness as a critic." When "the symbols of the myth become ... raw material that has to be fitted into a new context of meaning," an etiological chain is established and the mythic structure becomes reversed; rather than being taken for granted as grounded in the myth, social values are more or less consciously validated by mytho-speculative symbolization.[23]

Mytho-speculation is less stable and more subject to revision and annotation than myth because it raises the question of the meaning of existence itself. Questions of causation impel the story-teller to the divine ground. For example, when the Southern narrators of the Ham story asked why blacks should be enslaved, they were finally driven to God's will: blacks were enslaved because Ham, their father, was cursed by Noah; Ham was cursed by Noah because he had committed a heinous sin; Ham committed a heinous sin because he had a base character; Ham had a base character because he was created with an inferior intellect; Ham was created with an inferior intellect for some reason known fully only to God. Thus, the mytho-speculative symbolization in the Ham story was illumined by a religious formulation which stopped the questioning process; however, since the questioning process was introduced in the Ham myth in the first place, the religious illumination did not finally "assuage the unrest of the questioner," to quote Voegelin again. Hence myths (or more precisely "mytho-speculations") are never fully satisfactory for moderns in the same sense that "compact myths" are for those who have never questioned the meaning of existence itself. This does not mean, however, that the story of Ham did not function mythically, for it did synthesize otherwise incongruent features of the Southerners' world view and their ethos. "Mythopoeic extrapolation," according to Voegelin "does not break the form of the myth."[24]

Thus, the modern consciousness tends to make myths into mytho-speculations that are often explicitly allegorical (see pp. 130-31, above). The stories still function mythically and are expressed in mythic language, and as symbol systems they can be regarded as myths with one distinction: "Noetic consciousness," or "the life of reason," becomes "active within the medium of the cosmological myth."[25] Since Southerners began their mythic speculation with a questioning consciousness, they consciously adapted an originally compact myth into an explanation for black subordination and supposed racial differences. While the compact myth as found in Genesis 9 did not yield clear explanations of blackness or of chattel slavery (most probably it originally legitimized the Hebrews' conquest of Canaan), Southerners were able to make it fit through rational argumentation. However, since reason was injected into the mythic structure, the religious solution could not stand entirely on its own; rather, the religious explanation, which became grounded in the divine will, always raised further questions. Therefore, while the American versions of the Ham story at least partially resolved the Southerners' crisis of meaning symbolically and can thus be considered as myth, the symbolic coherence between world view and ethos forged by the story of Ham was not finally persuasive. Hence, exponents of the Ham myth buttressed it with more and more rational arguments; at times the myth became the framework for extremely lengthy treatises on racial differences and on the justice of enslaving blacks.[26]

* * *

But while the Ham story was more speculative and annotated than myths in traditional societies, it functioned as myth because it provided white Southerners with a symbolic framework for understanding their universe and legitimizing their racial values. By positing God's miraculous intervention in the family of Noah to differentiate three races of people, the story helped resolve tensions in the proslavery argument of Christians who held both that blacks should be enslaved and that they were fully human. Its narrative expression in language conveying the passive voice, the imperative mood, and the continuous progressive tense validated white beliefs about black inferiority, legitimized the blacks' enslavement as ordained by God, and prescribed the proper relationship that should always exist between blacks and whites.

Bronislav Malinowski writes that "myth fulfills in primitive culture an indispensable function: it expresses, enhances, and codifies belief; it safeguards and enforces morality; it vouches for the efficiency of ritual and contains practical rules for the guidance of man. Myth is thus a vital ingredient of human civilization...."[27] While the antebellum South was certainly not a "primitive" society according to ordinary anthropological definitions, the various versions of the Ham story functioned as do myths in traditional societies.

First, the Ham myth expressed, enhanced, and codified white beliefs about the nature of the black and white races. By establishing Ham, Shem, and Japheth as the archetypes for the black, red, and white races, the myth portrayed white racial attitudes: blacks were sensual, lascivious, and dull like their progenitor, Ham; Indians, while sexually modest, could not easily be converted to Christianity because their progenitor, Shem, had spurned it; whites were modest and intelligent like their progenitor, Japheth, who covered Noah and embraced the true religion.

Second, the myth enforced the morality of race relations in the antebellum South. By showing that black slavery was ordained by God through Noah's inspired proclamation, the myth validated black bondage in America. God's miraculous intervention in the family of Noah, establishing three distinct races with different temperaments and colors, indicated that amalgamation did not accord with the divine moral law; God had color-coded the races to show disapproval of miscegenation.

Third, the myth vouched for proper ritualistic attitudes between blacks and whites, thereby providing practical rules for the correct relationship between the races. According to evidence presented by Gunnar Myrdal, the customs of white supremacy (some of which became codified in "Jim Crow" laws in the late nineteenth century) were rooted in the antebellum period. Such customs and rituals as segregated seating in churches and the "ceremonial etiquette of obsequiousness" were common in the Old South.[28] The Ham myth enforced these rituals by clearly delineating the separate character traits of the black and white races and by showing that the "nature" of both races was predetermined by the character of their progenitors. A recent sociological study of white sects in the South by David Harrell evidences the Ham myth's continuing importance for those Southerners who interpret race relations in fundamentalist, biblical terms.[29] Therefore, the myth still justifies black subservience through such rituals as blacks' entering whites' homes through the rear door and remaining upright and hatless when conducting business with whites.

## NOTES

[1]This definition of myth is drawn from a variety of sources. On myth as narrative see especially Percy S. Cohen, "Theories of Myth," Man; The Journal of the Royal Anthropological Institute 4 (Sept. 1969), 349-53; and Paul Ricoeur, The Symbolism of Evil (1967; Boston: Beacon Press, 1969), pp. 162-72. On myth as irreducible to fact or fiction see especially Reinhold Niebuhr, "The Truth in Myths," The Nature of Religious Experience, ed. J. S. Bixler, R. L. Calhoun, and H. R. Niebuhr (New York: Harper & Brothers, 1937), passim; Mircea Eliade, Myth and Reality (1963; New York: Harper Torchbooks, 1968), pp. 5-8; Elizabeth Janeway, Man's World, Woman's Place: A Study in Social Mythology (New York: William Morrow, 1971), pp. 13, 26-47, 58, 295; and Ricoeur, pp. 163 ff.

Although I have inferred the linguistic part of the definition about mythic language from several sources, including those listed above, Janeway explicitly writes that myth is in the "imperative mood" (pp. 37, 40).

Although the "continuous progressive tense" is not recognized in standard English, linguists recognize its usage in "black English." The following example is from William Labov and Paul Cohen, "Systematic Relations of Standard and Non-Standard Rules in the Grammars of Negro Speakers," Language, Society, and Education: A Profile of Black English, ed. Johanna S. De Stefano (Worthington, Ohio: Charles A. Jones, 1973), p. 135: "They be fooling around" indicates "generality, repeated action, or existential state."

[2]Josiah Priest, Slavery (Albany, N.Y.: C. Van Benthuysen, 1843), p. 27.

[3]Priest, pp. 209-10.

[4]Priest, pp. 79-80.

[5]Claude Lévi-Strauss, Structural Anthropology (1958; New York: Basic Books, 1963), p. 209.

[6]Eliade, pp. 5-6.

[7]Cohen, pp. 349-52. See also Eliade, pp. 18-19; Ricoeur, pp. 163, 170-71.

[8]The second edition of Webster's New Twentieth Century Dictionary ... (World Pub. Co., 1956) lists "fable, fiction, legend, falsehood, invention" as synonyms for myth. The third edition, published in 1961, however, not only expands the use of "myth" but also avoids using "falsehood" in any of the definitions. Instead, "myth" is "a story invented as a veiled explanation for a truth," or "a person or thing existing only in imagination or whose actuality is not verifiable: as ... a belief given uncritical acceptance by the members of a group ... in support of existing or traditional practices and institutions ... [or] a belief or concept that embodies a visionary ideal."

[9]Stanley Meisler, "Efforts to Honor a Conqueror: An Unlikely Campaign in Mexico," San Francisco Chronicle, Sunday Punch Section, 10 Nov. 1974, p. 4.

[10]See Eliade, p. 6; and Niebuhr, passim.

[11]Clifford Geertz, The Interpretation of Cultures (New York: Basic Books, 1973), p. 112.

[12]James D. B. De Bow, "The Origin, Progress and Prospects of Slavery," De Bow's Review 9 (July 1850), 15; James D. B. De Bow, "Ethnological Researches--Is the African and Caucasian of Common Origin?" De Bow's Review 9 (Aug. 1850), 243-45.

[13]Thornton Stringfellow, Slavery (New York: J. F. Trow, 1861), p. 12.

[14]Stringfellow, pp. 34-35.

[15]Janeway, p. 28; see also pp. 26, 27, 295, 307; and Geertz, p. 112.

[16]For a particularly clear exposition see William James, "The Perception of Reality," The Principles of Psychology, 2 vols. (New York: Henry Holt, 1890), II, ch. 21.

[17]Peter L. Berger, The Sacred Canopy (1967; New York: Anchor Books of Doubleday, 1969), p. 45; see also Janeway, pp. 31-33.

[18]Berger, p. 138; see also pp. 31, 48-49, 151.

[19]Geertz, p. 127.

[20]Berger, p. 31.

[21]See pp. 72-73, 75, above.

[22]Robert Lewis Dabney, A Defense of Virginia (1867; rpt. New York: Negro Universities Press, 1969), pp. 102-3.

[23]Eric Voegelin, The Ecumenic Age, Order and History, vol. IV (Baton Rouge: Louisiana State University Press, 1974), pp. 64, 83, 317-20, and passim.

[24]Voegelin, pp. 59, 63, 67, 317, 320, 326-27, and passim.

[25]Voegelin, p. 67.

[26]Priest's work ran to 340 pages; Samuel Davies Baldwin's Dominion; or, The Unity and Trinity of the Human Race (Nashville: E. Stevenson and F. A. Owen, 1857) ran to 467 pages.

[27]Quoted in Eliade, p. 20.

[28]Gunnar Myrdal, An American Dilemma, 2 vols. (New York: Harper & Brothers, 1944), I, 577-78.

[29]David Edwin Harrell, Jr., White Sects and Black Men in the Recent South (Nashville: Vanderbilt University Press, 1971), pp. 60-61.

## Appendix

## ONE VERSION OF THE HAM MYTH

I have chosen to include the following anonymous version of the Ham myth for several reasons. First, the author tells the story comprehensively, without omitting or overemphasizing any of the major episodes. Second, unlike many versions, the author tells the story succinctly without too many digressions. Third, I discovered this pamphlet after I had completed most of my manuscript for this book and therefore I have not quoted any lengthy passages from it in previous chapters. Fourth, the style of this version has a higher literary quality than many others and is therefore very readable.

The episode reprinted here begins with the author's first paragraph and concludes where he begins to discuss the relationship between the Southern masters and their slaves. I have omitted the author's footnotes to his story since they are primarily digressions and add nothing but length to the account. Otherwise the text is complete. The author's anonymity, while frustrating from an historian's point of view, emphasizes that myths ultimately stand on their own as stories; the skill of the story-teller is more important than who he was.

The following selection is from *African Servitude: When, Why, and by Whom Instituted. By Whom, and How Long, Shall It be Maintained?* (New York: Davies & Kent, 1860), pp. 1-18.

## AFRICAN SERVITUDE

God, the Almighty, the Creator of the Heavens and the Earth, and the Righteous Governor of the Universe, did, in the beginning of the world, when He had prepared it for man's abode, make man in his own spiritual image; gave him full dominion of the earth, supplied his wants, and granted unto him free intercourse or communion with Him, his Creator and Benefactor; requiring of man obedience to his expressed commands.

Adam, the first man, deliberately broke the first command, by which act, and the spirit of disobedience he allowed in his heart, he fell from his high estate, hid, and cut himself off from communion with his God, and made both his body and soul subject to death.

The grievous offense of Adam against his Maker, God, the only source of light, life, and happiness in the universe, must of itself, according to the eternal laws of Truth and Order (whether God expressly said so or not), separate him from his Friend and Creator, causing the deliberate offender (unless reconciled) ever to recede from God, into the dark sea of misery and death.

The loss or death of all that was good and happy, and the knowledge or gain of all that was evil and miserable (the marks of which we all bear), are the results of the first offense.

Woman, the partner God had given to man, being the leader in the first great transgression, advises her husband to take part with her in it, and through her means he is deceived, and it seems in consequence thereof she fell from her state of equality with man--lost her equal right to counsel, judge, execute, and govern in the affairs of the world, and was worthily made subject to man or to her husband.

But this loss of woman is for time only, not for eternity, for the Redeemer of man finally restores all things to those who belong to Him.

God, in his goodness, adapted woman to her true position; gave her a will and heart to obey, and made the relation of husband and wife, in its true life or sense, desirable, happy, and blessed.

But woman's subjection to her husband hindereth not her happiness for time, or salvation for eternity; in fact, they are both promoted and secured in the exercise by her of a true spirit of obedience and submission to her condition and calling, and also by the discharge of the duties belonging to her, having faith in the appointed Saviour.

The family was instituted by God. In all its relations and results it is the most important, the happiest, and the most blessed institution with which He has endowed the human race.

He has placed great power and corresponding honor and responsibility on the united head of the family. For its use and influence God holds its head in a measure accountable to Him. The head of the family should teach its members to fear, love, and obey the Creator, who has the right, and ought to be, the God of every family. He has threatened to pour out His fury upon all the families that will not call upon His name.

The power or government that God has given to parents for a time, over the members of the family, is the most arbitrary known in the world; a government that the most powerful emperors and kings care not to intermeddle with.

The families of the old world became wicked and corrupt, it would seem, because the sons of God, or godly men, rejected the counsels of their fathers, and allied themselves with the wicked families of the earth, so that soon all were estranged from God. "Wickedness and violence filled the earth;" God determined, in his righteous judgment, to destroy the race. Noah, an honored patriarch, or ruler of a family, the ninth in descent from Adam, described as "a just man, perfect in his generations, walking with God," in the midst of the wicked and corrupt inhabitants of the earth, did find favor in the eyes, not of men, but of the Lord, and was informed of the flood of waters that God should "bring upon the earth, to destroy all flesh wherein is the breath of life from under heaven." Noah was instructed by Him to prepare an ark for the deliverance of himself and family when the deluge should come. He believed and obeyed the Lord, and with his wife and his three sons, with their wives, were preserved from the flood. These eight persons were monuments of God's saving mercy, and witnesses of His great power and righteous judgments.

The Patriarch Noah, being 600 years old, was now the head and father of the human family, the great representative of the race. He was the object of God's favor, and received from Him special and general directions for the government of the world.

So far as we can learn from the Bible, there was no human power or governor set up over the people higher than the patriarchal head or father of the family.

The Patriarchs were Rulers and Priests as well as Fathers. God is the author of all fatherhood, therefore children, or members of the family, must render to the head of it such obedience as the Lord requires.

The family government is truly the foundation of all other government, and it may yet, in the future, become the governing influence of the world. It may, in some respects, be a type of that one whole family in heaven and earth, mentioned by St. Paul in his Epistle to the Ephesians.

God is our Father in Heaven, and our Saviour teaches us to call Him so when we come to Him in prayer.

Noah became a husbandman, planted a vineyard, and, partaking too freely of the fruit of the vine, exposed himself to shame. The Scriptures do not state that he was guilty of anything more than an act of imprudence. In his exposed state he was discovered by his younger son, probably his grandson Canaan, who informed his father Ham, and one or both of them, so far from feeling or expressing grief for the dishonor of their parent, exultingly informed others of it, glorying in his shame, despising his power and authority, and his office as ruler and priest of God to them and the rest of their father's family, lightly esteeming also his parental blessing, as well as the blessing of God.

A true spirit of filial regard, love, honor, and obedience moved Shem and Japheth to protect their father; just the reverse of that which influenced their brother Ham to dishonor him. On the part of the former, it was an act of faith; of the latter, unbelief. The sin of Ham was not only great, but aggravated. He was probably more than six-score years old; for Canaan, his fourth son, all born after the flood, must have been old enough to discern between right and wrong, to have received the curse that fell upon him. Ham had seen the wickedness of the inhabitants of the old world, and knew they were destroyed because of their sins, which ought to have been a sufficient warning to him, not only to walk in the way of righteousness, but to command his family, and bring them up in the fear of the Lord, which it seems he did not do. He knew that God had chosen his father as the honored head of the human family, declaring him faithful, and communicating to him his designs. It was with Noah and his sons, including Ham, that God, after the flood, made or renewed with them his covenant, giving them and their posterity his promised blessing. In refusing to honor his parent, he refused to honor all governors, natural, civil, ecclesiastical, human, and divine. The sin was a representative one, and, under the circumstances, it was no light one in Ham and his son. It manifested in them no love for their parent, but an evil heart of unbelief toward God. For this offense the verdict of men and angels would at least be--that the disobedient should forfeit their rights and privileges, and be brought into subjection to the obedient. What the judgment of the Almighty was, we have recorded in his sure Word--Genesis ix. 24-28; and although the record is very brief, yet it is clear and plain to the candid mind. It states that Noah, after a full knowledge of all that had transpired--what his younger son had done unto him--said, "Cursed be Canaan; a servant of servants shall he be unto his brethren. And he said, Blessed be the Lord God of Shem, and Canaan shall be his servant. God shall enlarge Japheth, and he shall dwell in the tents of Shem, and Canaan shall be his servant."

In this instance, as in others, the curses as well as the blessings of the patriarchs are prophetical in their nature--to be fulfilled in future ages. This deliberate denunciation of Noah proceeded not from a spirit of indignation, but of prophecy. He was moved by the spirit of God to utter what he did--"For <u>the prophecy</u> came not in old time by the will of man, but holy men of God spake as they were moved by the Holy Ghost." As a prophet of the Lord, he foretold the consequences of the acts of his sons in this matter. The judgments that should follow the one, the blessings that should rest upon the others, as God, in His righteous will and pleasure, had seen fit to dispense, and which in time He would surely execute and fulfill.

It must be evident to every candid mind, that in this

brief prophetic annunciation of what should follow his posterity, that a condition of servitude is laid upon the children of Ham, especially upon Canaan; and that the posterity of Shem and Japheth should have the benefit of their service.

God, who knows the end from the beginning, and is acquainted with the hearts of all men, for wise purposes allowed the faith of the three sons of Noah to be tried, and Ham was found wanting. In consequences of his lack of faith, his sinful conduct or defection, and that of his family, the Judge of all the earth deprives him and his children from their equal position in the great human family, and in His righteous judgment determines that they shall be made subject to, or become servants to, the rest of the families of the earth. From that time forth, actual servitude of some sort became their normal condition--was, and is, the judicial law of their race. Our first parents broke the first command on the first table, by disobeying the true God, and obeying that usurper, the devil, the god of the world--the legal consequence of which was death of body and soul. Ham, the son of Noah, broke the first command on the second table, by scorning and deriding his father, the legal consequences of which seems to be death of his body, or the forfeiture of it for the benefit of others.

God's moral laws are ever the same, promulgated or not. The law of God, as given by Moses, states in Exodus xxi. 15th and 17th verses: "He that smiteth his father, or his mother, shall surely be put to death." "He that curseth his father, or his mother, shall surely be put to death."

James Fisher, the Scotch divine, in his comment, says: "This severe punishment was inflicted for these crimes because either beating or cursing of parents are sins directly opposite to the light and law of nature, and frequent evidences, not only of the worst kind of ingratitude, but of incurable disobedience; and, therefore, the equity of this punishment seems to be approved by our Lord, under the New Testament--Matt. xv. 4."

If the parent was guilty of neglect of duty, the guilt of the child would be less. It can not be said that Noah was guilty of neglect, for he was declared faithful in all his generations.

From the Word of God, there can be no doubt that for a time a condition of servitude was inflicted upon the descendants of Ham, in whole or in part--in all probability the whole. It may be said of Ham, that in Canaan his seed should be called. Poole, in his Annotations, states, that "Interpreters have invented several other reasons why the curse, which properly belonged to Ham, was inflicted on his son Canaan--as, 1st. When Canaan is mentioned, Ham is not exempted from the malediction, but rather more deeply plunged into it, because parents are apt to be more affected with their children's misfortunes than their own, especially if they themselves brought the evil upon them by their own fault or folly. 2d. God having blessed the three sons of Noah at their going out of the ark, it was not proper that Noah's curse should interfere with the Divine blessing, but very proper that it should be transferred to Canaan, in regard to the future extirpation of the people which were to descend from him. But--3d. Some imagine that there is here an ellipsis, or defect of the word father, since such relative words are frequently omitted, or understood, in Scripture. Thus, Matt. iv. 21: James of Zebedee, for *the son* of Zebedee. Acts vii. 16: Emmor of Sychem, for *the father* of Sychem, which our translation rightly supplies; and in like manner Canaan may be put for the father of Canaan, as the Arabic translation has it, i.e., Ham, as the Septuagint here renders it. And though Ham had more sons, yet he may here be described by his relation to Canaan, because in him the curse was more fixed and dreadful, reaching to his utter extirpation, while the rest of Ham's posterity in after-ages were blessed with the saving knowledge of the Gospel."

That there might not in after-ages be any mistake or doubt upon whom the curse was laid, it would seem that the Almighty put upon the descendants of Ham, not only the black mark of disobedience and condemnation to service, but also prepared and adapted both mind and body for the service required of them.

The fall, or defection of Ham, considered in all its results, is one of the most, if not the most, important event to the human race that has transpired since the flood; save, always, the advent and death of the Saviour, the great event of the universe.

Before this important event (the fall of Ham) it might be truly said that "all men were born free and equal" in rights and privileges, but after this curse, who shall say, in opposition to God's Word, that there is an equality in conditions, rights, and privileges of all the inhabitants of the earth?

To assert that all men are born free and equal in rights, privileges, and conditions, is to say what every man of common sense knows to be untrue. To assert that all men ought to be, is to call in question the wisdom and goodness of God. To say that all men will be, is to declare that which has not yet been revealed.

Let us take the history of the world as we find it recorded in the Bible and other approved books, and we shall find that this condition or dispensation of servitude resting upon the children of Ham, as far back as we have any authentic history of the race after the flood.

Those old patriarchs, Abraham, Isaac, and Jacob, had their servants, or bond men and women, in great numbers. A system of servitude had already, at that time, become a known and established condition in society.

We find, in times past, the prophetic declarations of the Patriarch Noah have been fulfilled, and that the curse and the blessing extend to our day, and are still in process of fulfillment according to God's sure Word.

The venerable Dr. Mede says: "There never has been a son of Ham who has shaken a scepter over the head of Japheth. Shem has subdued Japheth, and Japheth has subdued Shem, but Ham never subdued either."

That inspired servant of God and prototype of our Saviour, by the command of God, gave to the children of Israel the following permission, direction, and command, as found in Leviticus xxv. 44-46: "Both thy bondmen, and thy bondmaids, which thou shalt have, shall be of the heathen that are round about you; of them shall ye buy bondmen and bondmaids. Moreover, of the children of the strangers that do sojourn among you, of them shall ye buy, and of their families that are with you, which they begat in your land: and they shall be your possession. And ye shall take them as an inheritance for your children after you, to inherit them for a possession; they shall be your bondmen forever: but over your brethren the children of Israel, ye shall not rule one over another with rigor."

Here the Israelites have full permission from the

Almighty to buy, hold, and use forever the services of the heathen, or Canaanites, about them, who were descendants of Ham. Yet, we do not consider these texts, or this permission as the foundation for their right to hold these heathen as bond men and women forever. We consider this portion of Scripture as containing a new writ, or warrant of execution, for the services of the Canaanites, issued to Moses and the children of Israel by the great Judge of the earth, upon the old judgment rendered in the days of Noah, 850 years before.

Besides the directions given, these texts are valuable to us, because they show that God remembers His word, and will both perform it and accomplish His designs. The posterity of Shem are reminded of their right to the services of the descendants of Canaan. We, the children of Japheth, have also a right to the services of the descendants of Canaan, or Ham, according to that old, yet still living and abiding, dispensation of the Most High to the sons of Noah.

Shem and Japheth are not to blame for this condition of servitude abiding upon Ham; and if there is any advantage in receiving his service--as it seems there must be, for it is pronounced by Noah as a blessing--they have, for the honor and obedience they rendered to their parent, a right to it given them by the Almighty.

For reasons given in the preceding pages, we use promiscuously, as meaning or included in the same, the phrase, posterity of Ham, or descendants of Canaan. That the black race, or tribes of men inhabiting Africa, are the descendants of Ham, there can be no reasonable doubt, and it is not necessary to prove it here; in speaking of them, of the Africans, we shall consider that they are of the posterity of Ham, upon whom God has put his indelible mark, or _prima facie_ evidence, to all that they belong not to the posterity of Shem or Japheth.

We use the terms service, servitude, and servants, instead of slavery or slaves, as being more Scriptural, and conveying a true import or meaning of the prophetical curse and blessing under investigation. As to slavery, there is no slavery like sin; the devil only truly owns slaves, and if we are free from him, we are free indeed.

That verse--Gen. ix. 37--containing the important and comprehensive prediction concerning Japheth and Shem and

Canaan is rendered different from King James' version by some translators. One old translation, published about the year 1600 (before King James' version), renders the verse thus: "God persuade Japheth, that he may dwell in the tents of Shem, and let Canaan be his servant;" and the following is the marginal note of comment: "Or enlarge or cause to return." "He declareth that the Gentiles which came of Japheth, and were separated from the Church, should be joined to the same by the persuasion of God's spirit, and preaching of the Gospel." The above seems to convey, as far as it goes, a true purport or correct meaning of this most important prediction, and comprehensive one, as regards the period of time covered and the people involved. Bear in mind, that a blessing is pronounced on Shem and Japheth. It could be no blessing to Shem to have Japheth dwell in his tents, or hold and occupy his temporal possession. It seems more consistent with the whole passage to adopt the spiritual meaning, that Japheth shall, through the influence of God's spirit, receive and enjoy all the privileges and blessings of the Gospel, given first to Shem, though now lost or discarded by him. According to St. Paul--Rom. xi. 25--it shall be enjoyed by both when the fullness of the Gentiles be come in. The reasons and evidence that can be given in favor of this interpretation of the prophecy outweigh all others. This brings the fulfillment of the prophecy down to and through the Gospel ages. And there is no escaping the conclusion, that in the Gospel ages, or in the times when Japheth shall possess and enjoy the Gospel, then he shall also have Canaan to be his servant. What reasons can be given, or proof brought to show, that we ought to limit this prophecy--the blessing and the curse--to the days of the Israelites and Canaanites of old? We have as, as yet, seen none.

The interpretation advocated here of the true meaning of Gen. ix. 37 is supported by the events of time, by the workings of God's providences, which truly explain His predictions and unfold His designs:

"God's purposes will ripen fast,<br>
Unfolding every hour;<br>
The bud may have a bitter taste,<br>
But sweet will be the flower.<br>
Blind unbelief is sure to err,<br>
And scan His work in vain--<br>
God is His own interpreter,<br>
And He will make it plain."--Cowper.

In His Word it is written: "He hath done whatsoever He pleased, and He giveth not account of any of His matters". It does not become Him to stoop and explain His designs to carping mortals. His works of providence in time, and through eternity, do, and will, develop and explain all His plans, to His praise and the admiration of His creatures.

African servitude we hold, then, is not from man, but from God, dispensed in His wisdom and judgment to the posterity of Ham in consequence of sin. If it was a system of wrong and oppression, devised and maintained by the selfish will and power of men alone, it would not have stood a century, instead of reaching back over forty centuries, or more than one hundred generations. If the institution had its origin alone in the design or will of man, the righteous Governor of the world would have long since moved the so-called oppressed to have asserted their rights, achieved their freedom, and punished their adversaries.

We have no other resource, then, but to turn the whole matter over to the Almighty. Of ourselves we are not able to hold or maintain the system, but He is all-sufficient. Whatever good there is in the institution, ascribe to Him--the evil, take to ourselves.

If the system of servitude imposed upon the posterity of Ham is based upon God's purpose, as we believe it is, man can not overthrow it; and those who see good in it need not fear. There is no sufficient reason to believe God will release the posterity of Ham from the condition imposed until He has removed the mark of servitude He has put upon them.

As the preservation of the Jews as a separate people, though mingled for ages among all the nations of the earth, is considered a standing miracle, so we believe that this institution of bond-servants--this system of African servitude--will yet be considered a standing evidence of God's sovereign will and power, of His wisdom and goodness, and of the truth of His sure word and prophecy, of which our Saviour said that "He came not to destroy, but to fulfill;" and "till heaven and earth pass, one jot or tittle shall in no wise pass from the law till all be fulfilled."

Who shall complain because the Almighty, in His sovereign will and righteous judgment, saw fit for cause to lay upon a part of the human family a condition of servitude to the rest? "Will not the Judge of all the earth do right?"

Let us not teach any who are under the cloud to complain of any of the dispensations of God, and say, "Why hast Thou made me thus?" "As the potter has power over the clay to make of the same lump one vessel unto honor and another unto dishonor, so God can and will do with His creatures as He pleases, and none shall ever be able to charge Him with unrighteousness." God has the same right to condemn one portion of the race to servitude for a particular sin in the father, that He had in condemning the whole race to death for disobedience in the first parents of all. Who will have the hardihood to set his wisdom against that of the all-wise God, and say it is not good for the bodies or souls of men, for time or eternity, that men should be adjudged to labor, and earn their bread by the sweat of their brows? Who will put his kindness and consideration against the goodness and mercy of God, and say that it was not kind to *woman* that the Great Disposer of all should make her subject to her husband, and that her happiness and usefulness in this life were to be found in true and constant efforts to perform the duties of the station assigned her? And who shall say it is neither wise nor good for the African race (the descendants of Ham) to be in the service of other portions of the human family, and that the relation of master and servant is not alike necessary and beneficial to both? God can fit us for the station in life He intends we shall occupy, and give us such measure of intellect, strength of body, and power of endurance, that we shall be perfectly adapted to our condition or calling, and unfitted for any other. "As your day is, so shall your strength be." It is our duty with faith and patience to perform the duties of our condition or station in life, for therein lies our happiness and salvation.

When the earth was cursed for man's sake, we do not understand that any moral curse was put or charged upon it, but that it was in a measure deprived of those healthful or productive influences that should make it bear in abundance of all that was good, and only that which was good, for the living beings upon it.

So, when the posterity of Ham are cursed, we do not understand that a moral curse is pronounced upon and still hanging over them, but that they are made to stand lower in their position in the human family, and are deprived of their equality among their brethren of rights and privileges that they all before enjoyed in common; that there is nothing in the curse *per se* that prevents salvation, that hinders their coming to God through Jesus Christ. This state, or certain degree of servitude (now their normal condition), is not itself a barrier or preventive to their reception of the Gospel; and more than that, we hold to be true the doctrine, that submission to and rendering of the bond-service imposed upon the Africans (the posterity of Ham) actually tends to promote their well-being in this life and their eternal salvation.

We may believe that He who declared a soul to be of more value than the whole material world, would see to it that none of His dispensations to the human family should of themselves prove a hindrance to their salvation.

The righteous Governor of the world did and has sold his people Israel for short periods of time, and for generations, into the hands of wicked nations, because they turned away from, forgot, and disobeyed their Benefactor. Has He not the same right to dispose of the services of the degenerate children of a rebellious son to their more righteous brethren? If God in His wisdom sees fit to do this, as His Word declares He has done it, has, He not both the power and grace to adapt these degenerate children to the condition He has prepared for them? and can He not also, by His spirit, dispose those who receive these services of others, that they shall so deal with those, their servants, or bond men and women, that God's wisdom and mercy shall be praised, lives benefited, and souls saved? If it is better for woman, in view of time and eternity, to continue in the particular sphere marked out for her by God, rather than seek to fill some unnatural position not designed for her, why may it not be best for the African to occupy and perform (for time only) the duties belonging to a second-rate position in the human family, evidently assigned him by the Sovereign Disposer of all?

As the law of God (so just, yet so hard for us to obey) is a schoolmaster, to bring us to Christ the Saviour, so may not the condition of servitude be found necessary to bring those upon whom it is laid to the light, freedom, and salvation of the Gospel?

Do the facts concerning African servitude in this, our Gospel land, prove or lead us to believe that that condition tends to promote, more than any other, their temporal good and eternal happiness? We feel assured that they do. The fact that more than half a million of the colored population of the South are enrolled as members of the Evangelical churches, besides thousands who are not members, but seem to have and to exercise the faith of a true Christian, is an evident proof that there is a blessing somewhere for them in this institution, or dispensation, and that fruit thereof somehow grows from it unto eternal life.

On investigation it will be found, we believe, that a much larger proportion of the colored population of the South profess the Christian faith than in the free States at the North. And further, from all the information we have been able to gather, there is not much doubt but that the proportion of the colored population at the North at this time actually receiving and obeying the truths of the Gospel, is less than at the time when slavery was abolished in all the now free States of the Old Thirteen. At and before that time our New England fathers felt interested, and in a measure responsible for, the moral as well as physical well-being of their own servants, and taught them (as was the custom of many) the truths of the Gospel, and the doctrines as contained in their catechisms; they also, by proper restraint as well as example, caused their servants to obey, in a goodly measure, the precepts of the Bible.

From what we have personally seen at the South, we rejoice to know that multitudes of the Africans receive in simple faith the saving truths of the Gospel, and live contented and happy in the peaceful enjoyments of its hopes.

For example, take the city of Charleston, in South Carolina--(a state where the regulations concerning slavery, or bond-servants, are the most stringent, as are generally admitted)--in that city we have seen, in the morning, afternoon, and evening of the Sabbath days, summer and winter, the large galleries of the churches belonging to the Methodist, Baptist, Presbyterian, and Episcopal denominations, particularly the former, filled to overflowing with the colored population of that city, drinking in with joy the water of life that flows from those wells of salvation. They hear, seem fully to understand, believe, receive, and rejoice in the Gospel, which is as faithfully preached in the churches of that city, and at the South, as it is at the North. In that city we have been deeply impressed with the truth and preciousness of that blessing pronounced by the Redeemer, when He said, "Blessed be ye poor, for yours is the kingdom of God."

In no part of our country are the laboring population better provided and cared for than the African race at the

South. If we believed that the system of African servitude, in its best and true sense, hindered the salvation of their souls, we could not defend it. But we believe the reverse--that the burden that is laid upon them is meant and works for their good.

Those acquainted with the African character know that they do not possess that power of reason, soundness of judgment, strength of resolution; that perseverance, and nerved and fixed purpose of mind, stability of character, and power to resist evil influences and temptations, that are possessed by the whites; but that in faith and love, in honest simplicity, frank expression of feelings, they are equal to the other races; and that in contentment, docility, meekness, patience, and power of endurance, they excel the whites.

These prominent and important traits of character fit them for the important place, and that only, though a subordinate one, that God intended they should occupy, as we learn from his Word and providence. From their service the whites receive (and that with a good conscience) a certain measure of comfort and prosperity. The posterity of Ham, in living among the whites and rendering service to them (especially in our country), have an enhanced degree of health, length of life, comfort, security, quietness, freedom from care, and a participation in the blessings of the Gospel, as dispensed in our land. They have, also (singular though it may seem, yet generally a fact), a degree of pride and satisfaction in the prosperity of their masters, enhanced as it has been by their services--a sort of consciousness "that they have done what they could." "The sleep of the laboring man is sweet, whether he eat little or much," said the wise man. (He who made all things well, made it so that the laboring man should take his portion and rejoice in his labor.)

It is asserted that the system of slavery, or African servitude, in any degree is cruel and unjust. Those who are best acquainted with the system in our Southern States do not believe it, and know that it is not necessarily so, and that there are no evils connected with it but that might all be remedied.

It is charged that the masters of the Africans are naturally inclined to ill-treat and oppress them. The rule is just the reverse. It is proverbial that the white overseer at the South is more kind and compassionate than the black overseer. The white man is more lenient, and endures with patience the stupidity, obstinacy, and laziness of the black servant more than he does any other class.

The renowned and learned Calmet wrote near one hundred and fifty years ago, that "'Tis a tradition among the Eastern writers, that Noah, having cursed Ham and Canaan, the effect of his curse was, that not only their posterity were made subject to their brethren and born, as we may say, in slavery, but that likewise all on a sudden the color of their skin became black (for these Eastern writers maintain that all the blacks descended from Ham and Canaan); that Noah, seeing so surprising a change, was deeply affected with it, and begged of God that He would be pleased to inspire Canaan masters with a tender and compassionate love for him, and that his prayer was heard. For notwithstanding we may still at this day observe the effect of Noah's curse in the servitude of Ham's posterity, yet we may remark likewise the effect of his prayer, in that this sort of black slave is sought for and made much of in most places."--Calmet's Dictionary, on the word Ham.

The fact that Noah thus prayed rests, as some will maintain, upon tradition only. Admit it. We know that as a father he would pity his children; that as a good and righteous man he would intercede and pray for them, and that the prayer-hearing God would hear, and, as far as He thought best, alleviate the curse, and bring good out of it.

It is, in fact, owing to this natural feeling of compassion for the blacks, possessed in a measure by the whites (implanted within them by their Maker), that we have such a disposition to sympathize with them in their state of servitude, so that we allow our natural feelings of kindness to go too far or take a wrong direction, seeking present deliverance for the body only, by abolishing or null[if]ying this condition of servitude, when God's providence and our practical experience do not favor it, nor his Word require it, nor the happiness and welfare of the blacks demand it.

In the practical exercise of the principles of true benevolence--of love and charity--it is not certain that it is the will of God that we should put forth effort to change the calling of any class of men; but the opposite seems to be true. It is our duty and privilege to do good, as we have opportunity, to all classes of men in their present calling or condition. If we bend all our efforts to change the calling of men, and not to improve them in their present condition, we at least seemingly work against God's providence, worse than waste our energies, and bring about a disturbed and injurious state of affairs. It is better, as the inspired St. Paul wrote, "That every man abide in the same calling wherein he was called." "For he that is called in the Lord, being a servant, is the Lord's freeman; likewise also he that is called, being free, is Christ's servant. Let every man wherein he is called therein abide."

Would it not be the part of wisdom in all those who are laboring to change the calling or relieve the African race from the condition of servitude resting upon them, to hesitate and stop, until they find and produce from God's Word undoubted support and authority for their acts.

A careful examination of the past history of the white and black races, and of the opinions and acts of the mass of the people of the present day, make it evident to all who are willing to draw legitimate conclusions on the subject, that the two races can not live quietly and harmoniously together in a state of EQUALITY. For peace' sake, the black must give place to the white, or in some way come under a condition of servitude to him. Even now the legislatures of many of our States are pressed by the people to pass laws expelling the free blacks, or preventing their settlement within the bounds of the State.

But there is no difficulty or disturbance in those communities where the blacks take their true position, and are in a certain degree in subjection to the whites. From the history of the African race there is abundant proof that they thrive not well alone, separated from the white races. Alone they make no progress in civilization, arts, and commerce. They can not maintain, and so can not reap, the benefits of free constitutional governments. They are enslaved and bound down to vice, crime, and misery. The Africans seem not able to stand alone among the nations, or to live intermingled among other nations, only as they are in some degree subservient to them.

As the vine twines about the oak for support, so the black loves to dwell near the white, and enjoy the security and support there is in his presence. When he is in his proper place, there is a mutual and reciprocal feeling of love and dependence that tends to promote the comfort and happiness of both. "The strong ought to bear the weak."

It certainly seems that God intended the races should dwell together in the relations He appears to have ordained.

Many have wondered why the colored population refuse to immigrate, and establish free governments and institutions by themselves in Africa. Thousands refuse to go, even when they may have freedom from American slavery by going. To the Africans, the thought of going to Africa is generally repugnant. Is it not because the Almighty has, in His wisdom, designed it otherwise; and may He not hold that great continent yet in reserve, to be occupied by the posterity of Shem and Japheth, in connection with that of Ham?

## BIBLIOGRAPHY

### PRIMARY SOURCES

"Africa in America," Southern Literary Messenger 22 (Jan. 1856), 1-9.

African Servitude: When, Why, and by Whom Instituted. By Whom, and How Long Shall It Be Maintained. New York: Davies & Kent, 1860.

Bachman, John. The Doctrine of the Unity of the Human Race Examined on the Principles of Science. Charleston: C. Canning, 1850.

Baldwin, Samuel Davies. Dominion; or, The Unity and Trinity of the Human Race; With the Divine Political Constitution of the World, and the Divine Rights of Shem, Ham and Japheth. Nashville: Printed by E. Stevenson and F. A. Owen, 1857.

Barnes, Albert. An Inquiry into the Scriptural Views of Slavery. 1857; rpt. New York: Negro Universities Press, 1969.

"The Black Race in North America; Why Was Their Introduction Permitted?" Southern Literary Messenger 21 (Nov. 1855), 641-84.

Blyden, Edward W. "The Call of Providence to the Descendants of Africa in America," Negro Social and Political Thought 1850-1920: Representative Texts. Ed. Howard Brotz. New York: Basic Books, 1966, 112-26.

[Brookes, Iveson L.]. A Defence of Southern Slavery Against the Attacks of Henry Clay and Alex'r Campbell. Hamburg, S.C.: Robinson and Carlisle, 1851.

_______. A Defence of the South against the Reproaches and

Incroachments of the North: In Which Slavery Is Shown to Be an Institution of God Intended to Form the Basis of the Best Social State and the Only Safeguard to the Permanence of a Republican Government. Hamburg, S.C.: The Republican Office, 1850.

Brownlow, William Gannaway, and Abram Pryne. Ought American Slavery to Be Perpetuated? A Debate between Rev. W. G. Brownlow and Rev. A. Pryne. Held at Philadelphia, September, 1858. 1858; rpt. Miami: Mnemosyne Pub. Co., 1969.

Calhoun, John Caldwell. The Works of John C. Calhoun. Ed. Richard K. Crallé. 6 vols., 1851-1856; New York: D. Appleton and Company, 1888.

Calmet, Augustin. Calmet's Dictionary of the Holy Bible: Historical, Critical, Geographical and Etymological: Wherein Are Explained All the Proper Names in the Old and New Testament. Ed. Charles Taylor. London: W. Stratford, Crown-Court, Temple-Bar, 1800.

________. Fragments, Being Illustrations of the Manners, Incidents, and Phraseology of Holy Scripture ... Intended as a Continued Appendix to Calmet's Dictionary of the Holy Bible. 2nd ed. Ed. Charles Taylor. London: W. Stratford, Crown-Court, Temple-Bar, 1801.

Campbell, John. Negro-Mania: Being an Examination of the Falsely Assumed Equality of the Various Races of Men; Demonstrated by the Investigations of Champollion, Wilkinson, Rosellini, Van-Amringe, Gliddon, Young, Morton, Knox, Lawrence, Gen. J. H. Hammond, Murray, Smith, W. Gilmore Simms, English, Conrad, Elder, Prichard, Blumenbach, Cuvier, Brown, Le Vaillant, Carlyle, Cardinal Wiseman, Burckhardt, and Jefferson. Together with a Concluding Chapter, Presenting a Comparative Statement of the Condition of the Negroes in the West Indies before and since Emancipation. 1851; rpt. Miami: Mnemosyne Pub. Co., 1969.

Cartwright, Samuel Adolphus. "Canaan Identified with the Ethiopian," Southern Quarterly Review 2 (Oct. 1842), 321-83.

________. "Diseases and Peculiarities of the Negro Race, Part 1," De Bow's Review 11 (July 1851), 64-69.

________. "Diseases and Peculiarities of the Negro Race, Part 3," De Bow's Review 11 (Sept. 1851), 331-36.

________. "Dr. Cartwright on the Caucasians and the Africans," De Bow's Review 25 (July 1858), 45-56.

________. Essays, Being Inductions Drawn from the Baconian Philosophy Proving the Truth of the Bible and the Justice and Benevolence of the Decree Dooming Canaan to Be Servant of Servants: And Answering the Question of Voltaire: "On Demande Quel Droit des Etrangers tels que les Juifs Avaient sur le Pays de Canaan?" in a Series of Letters to the Rev. William Winans. Vidalia, La.: n.p., 1843.

________. "How to Save the Republic, and the Position of the South in the Union," De Bow's Review 11 (Aug. 1851), 184-97.

Channing, William Ellery. "Slavery," The Works of William E. Channing, D. D. Boston: American Unitarian Association, 1878, 688-743.

"Channing's Duty of the Free States," Southern Quarterly Review 2 (1842), 130-77.

Christy, David. "Cotton Is King: Or Slavery in the Light of Political Economy," Cotton Is King, and Pro-Slavery Arguments: Comprising the Writings of Hammond, Harper, Christy, Stringfellow, Hodge, Bledsoe, and Cartwright, on This Important Subject. Ed. E. N. Elliott. Augusta, Ga.: Pritchard, Abbott & Loomis, 1860, 19-267.

A Citizen of Georgia. Remarks upon Slavery; Occasioned by Attempts Made to Circulate Improper Publications in the Southern States. Augusta: S. R. Sentinel Office, 1835.

Clarkson, A. "The Basis of Northern Hostility to the South," De Bow's Review 28 (Jan. 1860), 7-16.

Cobb, Howell. A Scriptural Examination of the Institution of Slavery in the United States; with Its Objects and

*Purposes*. 1856; rpt. New York: Books for Libraries Press, 1972.

Cobb, Thomas R. R. *An Inquiry into the Law of Negro Slavery in the United States of America. To Which Is Prefixed an Historical Sketch of Slavery*. 1858; rpt. New York: Negro Universities Press, 1968.

Colfax, Richard H. *Evidence against the Views of the Abolitionists, Consisting of Physical and Moral Proofs, of the Natural Inferiority of the Negroes*. New York: James T. M. Bleakley, 1833.

Dabney, Robert Lewis. "Christians, Pray for Your Country," *Discussions by Robert L. Dabney, D. D., LL. D., Professor of Moral Philosophy in the University of Texas, and for Many Years Professor of Theology in Union Theological Seminary in Virginia*. Vol. II, *Evengelical*. Ed. C. R. Vaughan. Richmond: Presbyterian Committee of Publication, 1891, 393-400.

________. *A Defense of Virginia, and through Her of the South, in Recent and Pending Contests against the Sectional Party*. 1867; rpt. New York: Negro Universities Press, 1969.

Dagg, John Leadley. *The Elements of Moral Science*. 1859; New York: Sheldon & Company, 1860.

Dalcho, Frederick. *Practical Considerations Founded on the Scriptures, Relative to the Slave Population of South Carolina*. Charleston: A. E. Miller, 1823.

De Bow, James D. B. "The Earth and Its Indigenous Races," *De Bow's Review* 23 (July 1857), 70-77.

________. "[Editorial Introduction to] Harper's Memoir on Slavery," *De Bow's Review* 8 (March 1850), 232.

________. "Ethnological Researches--Is the African and Caucasian of Common Origin?" *De Bow's Review* 9 (Aug. 1850), 243-45.

________. "The Non-Slaveholders of the South," *De Bow's Review* 30 (Jan. 1861), 67-77.

________. "The Origin, Progress and Prospects of Slavery," *De Bow's Review* 9 (July 1850), 9-19.

Dew, Thomas Roderick. "Professor Dew on Slavery" SEE The Pro-Slavery Argument.

Douglass, Frederick. Life and Times of Frederick Douglass. 1892; New York: Bonanza Books, 1962.

England, John. "Letters to the Hon. John Forsyth, on the Subject of Domestic Slavery; to Which Are Prefixed Copies, in Latin and English, of the Pope's Apostolic Letter Concerning the African Slave Trade, with Some Introductory Remarks, etc.," The Works of the Right Rev. John England, First Bishop of Charleston, Collected and Arranged under the Advice and Direction of His Immediate Successor, the Right Rev. Ignatius Aloysius Reynolds, and Printed for Him, in Five Volumes. Baltimore: John Murphy & Co., 1849, III, 106-91.

Estes, Matthew. A Defence of Negro Slavery, as It Exists in the United States. Montgomery: Press of the "Alabama Journal," 1846.

Ewart, David. A Scriptural View of the Moral Relations of African Slavery. 1849; Charleston: Walker, Evans & Co., 1859.

Filmer, Robert. Patriarcha and Other Political Works of Sir Robert Filmer. Ed. and Intro. Peter Laslett. Oxford: Basil Blackwell, 1949.

Fitzhugh, George. "The Black and White Races of Men," De Bow's Review 30 (April 1861), 446-56.

________. Cannibals All! or, Slaves without Masters. Ed. Comer Vann Woodward. 1857; Cambridge, Mass.: Belknap Press of Harvard University Press, 1960.

________. "The Counter Current, or Slavery Principle," De Bow's Review 21 (July 1856), 90-95.

________. Slavery Justified; by a Southerner. Fredericksburg, Va.: Recorder Printing Office, 1850.

________. Sociology for the South; or, the Failure of Free Society. 1854; rpt. New York: Burt Franklin, 1965.

________. "Southern Thought," De Bow's Review 23 (Oct. 1857), 337-49.

________. "Southern Thought Again," De Bow's Review 23 (Nov. 1857), 449-61.

Fletcher, John. Studies on Slavery, in Easy Lessons: Compiled into Eight Studies, and Subdivided into Short Lessons for the Convenience of Readers. Natchez, Miss.: Jackson Warner, 1852.

Flournoy, John J. An Essay on the Origin, Habits & c. of the African Race: Incidental to the Propriety of Having Nothing to Do with Negroes: Addressed to the Good People of the United States. New York: n.p., 1835.

Freeman, Frederick. Africa's Redemption the Salvation of Our Country. New York: D. Fanshaw, 1852.

Fuller, Richard, and Francis Wayland. Domestic Slavery Considered as a Scriptural Institution: In a Correspondence between the Rev. Richard Fuller, of Beaufort, S.C., and the Rev. Francis Wayland, of Providence, R.I. 5th ed., New York: Sheldon Lamport & Blakeman, 1856.

Garnett. "The South and the Union," De Bow's Review 19 (July 1855), 38-47.

Grayson, William J. "The Hireling and the Slave," De Bow's Review 21 (Sept. 1856), 248-56.

Guenebault, J. H., ed. Natural History of the Negro Race, Extracted from the French [of J. T. Virey]. Charleston: D. J. Dowling, 1837.

Hamilton, William Thomas. The "Friend of Moses"; or, A Defence of the Pentateuch as the Production of Moses and an Inspired Document, against the Objections of Modern Skepticism. New York: M. W. Dodd, 1852.

Hammond, James Henry. "Hammond's Letters on Slavery" SEE The Pro-Slavery Argument.

________. Remarks of Mr. Hammond, of South Carolina, on the Question of Receiving Petitions for the Abolition of Slavery in the District of Columbia. Delivered in the House of Representatives, February 1, 1836. Washington City [sic; D.C.]: Duff Green, 1836.

Harper, William. "Harper on Slavery" SEE The Pro-Slavery Argument.

Helper, Hinton Rowan. The Impending Crisis of the South: How to Meet It. Ed. George M. Fredrickson. 1857; Cambridge, Mass.: Belknap Press of Harvard University Press, 1968.

________. The Negroes in Negroland; The Negroes in America; And Negroes Generally. Also, the Several Races of White Men, Considered as the Involuntary and Predestined Supplanters of the Black Races. New York: George W. Carleton, 1868.

________. Nojoque: A Question for a Continent. New York: George W. Carleton, 1867.

Holland, Edwin Clifford. A Refutation of the Calumnies Circulated against the Southern and Western States, Respecting the Institution and Existence of Slavery among Them. To Which Is Added a Minute and Particular Account of the Actual State and Condition of Their Negro Population. Together with Historical Notices of All the Insurrections That Have Taken Place since the Settlement of the Country. Charleston: A. E. Miller, 1822.

Hunter, Robert Mercer Taliaferro. "Mr. Hunter on the English Negro Apprentice Trade," De Bow's Review 24 (June 1858), 492-502.

Jefferson, Thomas. Notes on the State of Virginia. Intro. Thomas Perkins Abernethy. 1861; New York: Harper Torchbooks, 1964.

Johnson, Reverdy. Slavery. Its Institution and Origin. Its Status under the Law and under the Gospel. Its Agricultural, Commercial, and Financial Aspects. N.p., n.d.

Ker, Leander. Slavery Consistent with Christianity; With an Introduction, Embracing a Notice of the "Uncle Tom's Cabin" Movement in England. 3rd ed. Weston, Mo.: Finch & O'Gorman, Reporter Office, 1853.

Lord, Nathan. A Letter of Inquiry to Ministers of the Gospel of All Denominations, on Slavery, by a Northern

Presbyter. Boston: Little, Brown, and Co., 1854.

_______. A Northern Presbyter's Second Letter to Ministers of the Gospel of All Denominations on Slavery. Boston: Little, Brown, and Co., 1855.

M., L. S. "Negromania," De Bow's Review 12 (May 1852), 507-24.

McCaine, Alexander. Slavery Defended from Scripture, against the Attacks of the Abolitionists, in a Speech Delivered before the General Conference of the Methodist Protestant Church, in Baltimore, 1842. Baltimore: Printed by Wm. Wooddy, 1842.

Meigs, J. Aitken. "The Cranial Characteristics of the Races of Man," Indigenous Races of the Earth; or, New Chapters of Ethnological Inquiry; Including Monographs on Special Departments of Philology, Iconography, Cranioscopy, Palaeontology, Pathology, Archaeology, Comparative Geography, and Natural History. Ed. Josiah C. Nott and George R. Gliddon. Philadelphia: J. B. Lippincott & Co., 1857, 203-352.

Meisler, Stanley. "Efforts to Honor a Conqueror: An Unlikely Campaign in Mexico," San Francisco Chronicle, Sunday Punch Section, 10 Nov. 1974, p. 4.

Mell, Patrick H. Slavery: A Treatise, Showing That Slavery Is Neither a Moral, Political, Nor Social Evil. Penfield, Ga.: Benj. Brantley, 1844.

A Mississippian. "Slavery--The Bible and the 'Three Thousand Parsons.'" De Bow's Review 26 (Jan. 1859), 43-51.

Mitchell, J. C. A Bible Defence of Slavery and the Unity of Mankind. Mobile: J. Y. Thompson, 1861.

Newton, Thomas. Dissertations on the Prophecies, Which Have Remarkably Been Fulfilled, and at This Time Are Fulfilling in the World. 2nd ed. 3 vols. London: J. and R. Tonson, 1759.

Nott, Josiah Clark. An Essay on the Natural History of Mankind, Viewed in Connection with Negro Slavery:

Delivered before the Southern Rights Association, 14th December, 1850. Mobile: Dade, Thompson & Co., 1851.

________. "Statistics of Southern Slave Population; with Especial Reference to Life Insurance," De Bow's Review 4 (Nov. 1847), 275-89.

________. Two Lectures on the Connection between the Biblical and Physical History of Man. Delivered by Invitation, from the Chair of Political Economy, etc., of the Louisiana University, in December, 1848. 1849; rpt. New York: Negro Universities Press, 1969.

________ and George R. Gliddon. Types of Mankind: or, Ethnological Researches, Based upon the Ancient Monuments, Paintings, Sculptures, and Crania of Races, and upon Their Natural, Geographical, Philological, and Biblical History. Philadelphia: Lippincott, Grambo, 1854.

Pennington, James W. C. A Text Book of the Origin and History, &c. &c. of the Colored People. Hartford: L. Skinner Printer, 1841.

Pickens, Francis Wilkenson. Speech of Mr. Pickens, of South Carolina, in the House of Representatives, January 21, 1836, on the Abolition Question. Washington: Gales & Seaton, 1836.

Priest, Josiah. Slavery, as It Relates to the Negro, or African Race, Examined in the Light of Circumstances, History and the Holy Scriptures; with an Account of the Origin of the Black Man's Color, Causes of his State of Servitude and Traces of His Character as Well in Ancient as in Modern Times. Albany, N.Y.: C. Van Benthuysen & Co., 1843.

The Pro-Slavery Argument; As Maintained by the Most Distinguished Writers of the Southern States, Containing the Several Essays, on the Subject, of Chancellor Harper, Governor Hammond, Dr. Simms, and Professor Dew. 1852; rpt. New York: Negro Universities Press, 1968, 175-285.

R., H. O. The Governing Race: A Book for the Time, and

*for All Times*. Washington, D.C.: Thomas McGill, 1860.

Rankin, John. *Letters on American Slavery, Addressed to Mr. Thomas Rankin, Merchant at Middlebrook, Augusta Co., Va.* 1837; rpt. Westport, Conn.: Negro Universities Press, 1970.

Reed, Thomas. "Unity of Mankind," *De Bow's Review* 30 (April 1861), 407-9.

Rice, David. "Racial Mixture and Slavery," *Racial Thought in America*. Vol. I, *From the Puritans to Abraham Lincoln: A Documentary History*. Ed. Louis Ruchames. New York: Universal Library, Grosset & Dunlap, 1970, 226-27.

Roane, A. J. "Moral and Intellectual Diversity of the Races," *De Bow's Review* 21 (July 1856), 63-70.

———. "Reply to Abolition Objections to Slavery," *De Bow's Review* 20 (June 1856), 645-70.

———. "Ross on Slavery and Stiles' Modern Reform," *De Bow's Review* 24 (April 1858), 304-12.

Robinson, John Bell. *Pictures of Slavery and Anti-Slavery. Advantages of Negro Slavery and the Benefits of Negro Freedom, Morally, Socially, and Politically Considered*. 1863; rpt. Miami: Mnemosyne Pub. Co., 1969.

Robinson, Solon. "Negro Slavery at the South," *De Bow's Review* 7 (Sept. 1849), 206-25.

Ross, Frederick Augustus. *Slavery Ordained of God*. 1857; rpt. Miami: Mnemosyne Pub. Co., 1969.

Ruffin, Edmund. "Equality of the Races--Haytien and British Experiments," *De Bow's Review* 25 (July 1858), 27-38.

Sawyer, George S. *Southern Institutes; or, An Inquiry into the Origin and Early Prevalence of Slavery and the Slave Trade*. 1859; rpt. Miami: Mnemosyne Pub. Co., 1969.

Schaff, Philip. *Slavery and the Bible. A Tract for the Times*. Chambersburg, Pa.: M. Kieffer & Co., 1861.

Sewall, Samuel. "The Selling of Joseph: A Memorial," Racial Thought in America. Vol. I, From the Puritans to Abraham Lincoln: A Documentary History. Ed. Louis Ruchames. New York: Universal Library, Grosset & Dunlap, 1970, 47-52.

Shortridge, George D. "Mr. Jefferson--The Declaration of Independence and Freedom," De Bow's Review 26 (May 1859), 547-59.

Simms, William Gilmore. "The Morals of Slavery" SEE The Pro-Slavery Argument.

Sloan, James A. The Great Question Answered; or, Is Slavery a Sin in Itself (Per Se?) Answered According to the Teaching of the Scriptures. Memphis: Hutton, Gallaway & Co., 1857.

Smith, William A. Lectures on the Philosophy and Practice of Slavery, as Exhibited in the Institution of Domestic Slavery in the United States: With the Duties of Masters and Slaves. Nashville: Stevenson & Evans, 1856.

Smyth, Thomas. The Unity of the Human Races Proved to Be the Doctrine of Scripture, Reason and Science: With a Review of the Present Position and Theory of Professor Agassiz (1851). Complete Works of Rev. Thomas Smyth, D. D. Ed. J. William Flinn. 10 vols., Columbia, S.C.: R. L. Bryan Co., 1910, VIII, 5-392.

Stephens, Alexander Hamilton. "Speech Delivered on the 21st March, 1861, in Savannah, Known as 'The Corner Stone Speech,' Reported in the Savannah Republican," Alexander H. Stephens, in Public and Private. With Letters and Speeches, before, during, and since the War. Ed. Henry Cleveland. Philadelphia: National Pub. Co., 1866, 717-729.

________. "Speech on the Wilmot Proviso," Alexander H. Stephens, in Public and Private. With Letters and Speeches, before, during, and since the War. Ed. Henry Cleveland. Philadelphia: National Pub. Co., 1866, 86-88.

Stowe, Harriet Beecher. Uncle Tom's Cabin: Or, Life among the Lowly. 1852; New York: Harper & Row, 1965.

Stringfellow, Thornton. Scriptural and Statistical Views in Favor of Slavery. 1841; 4th ed., Richmond: J. W. Randolph, 1856.

________. Slavery: Its Origin, Nature, and History, Considered in the Light of Bible Teachings, Moral Justice, and Political Wisdom. New York: J. F. Trow, Printer, 1861.

Thrasher, John B. Slavery a Divine Institution. A Speech Made before the Breckinridge and Lane Club, November 5th, 1860. Port Gibson, Miss.: Southern Reveille Book and Job Office, 1861.

Toombs, Robert. "Slavery: Its Constitutional Status, and Its Influence on Society and the Colored Race," De Bow's Review 20 (May 1856), 581-605.

Tucker, George. The History of the United States, from Their Colonization to the End of the Twenty-Sixth Congress, in 1841. Philadelphia: J. B. Lippincott & Co., 1856-1858.

Twain, Mark. Pudd'nhead Wilson. 1894; New York: Grove Press, 1955.

Van Evrie, John H. Negroes and Negro "Slavery": The First an Inferior Race. The Latter Its Normal Condition. 3rd ed., 1863; rpt. Miami: Mnemosyne Publishing Co., 1969.

Verot, Augustin. A Tract for the Times. Slavery and Abolitionism, Being the Substance of a Sermon, Preached in the Church of St. Augustine, Florida, on the 4th Day of January, 1861, Day of Public Humiliation, Fasting and Prayer. New Orleans: n.p., 1861.

Wayland, Francis. The Elements of Moral Science. Boston: Gould and Lincoln, 1870.

Weld, Theodore Dwight. The Bible against Slavery. An Inquiry into the Patriarchal and Mosaic Systems on the Subject of Human Rights. 3rd ed., New York: American Anti-Slavery Society, 1838.

Woolman, John. "Some Considerations on the Keeping of

Negroes," Journal and Essays of John Woolman. Ed. Amelia M. Gummere. 1774; New York: Macmillan Co., 1922, 348-81.

SECONDARY SOURCES

Berger, Peter L. The Sacred Canopy: Elements of a Sociological Theory of Religion. 1967; New York: Doubleday Anchor Books, 1969.

Blassingame, John W. The Slave Community: Plantation Life in the Antebellum South. New York: Oxford University Press, 1972.

Cash, Wilbur J. The Mind of the South. 1929; New York: Vintage Books, 1941.

Clebsch, William A. From Sacred to Profane America: The Role of Religion in American History. New York: Harper & Row, 1968.

Cohen, Percy S. "Theories of Myth," Man: The Journal of the Royal Anthropological Institute 4 (Sept. 1969), 337-53.

Craven, Avery O. The Growth of Southern Nationalism 1848-1861. Vol. VI of A History of the South, ed. W. H. Stephenson and E. M. Coulter. Baton Rouge: Louisiana State University Press, 1953.

Davis, David Brion. The Problem of Slavery in the Age of Revolution 1770-1823. Ithaca, N.Y.: Cornell University Press, 1975.

______. The Problem of Slavery in Western Culture. Ithaca, N.Y.: Cornell University Press, 1966.

Doherty, Herbert J., Jr. "The Mind of the Antebellum South," Writing Southern History: Essays in Historiography in Honor of Fletcher M. Green. Ed. Arthur S. Link and Rembert W. Patrick. Baton Rouge: Louisiana State University Press, 1965.

Dollard, John. Caste and Class in a Southern Town. 3rd ed., 1937; New York: Doubleday Anchor Books, 1949.

Eaton, Clement. The Growth of Southern Civilization 1790-1860. New York: Harper & Brothers, 1961.

________. A History of the Old South. New York: Macmillan, 1949.

________. The Mind of the Old South. Baton Rouge: Louisiana State University Press, 1967.

Eliade, Mircea. Myth and Reality. 1963; New York: Harper Torchbooks, 1968.

Fredrickson, George M. Black Image in the White Mind: The Debate on Afro-American Character and Destiny, 1817-1914. 1971; New York: Harper Torchbooks, 1972.

Geertz, Clifford. The Interpretation of Cultures: Selected Essays. New York: Basic Books, 1973.

Genovese, Eugene D. Roll Jordan Roll: The World the Slaves Made. 1972; New York: Random House Vintage Books, 1976.

Ginzberg, Louis. The Legends of the Jews. 7 vols., Philadelphia: Jewish Publication Society of America, 1909-1938.

Greenberg, Kenneth S. "Revolutionary Ideology and the Proslavery Argument: The Abolition of Slavery in Antebellum South Carolina." The Journal of Southern History 42 (Aug. 1976), 365-84.

Harrell, David Edwin, Jr. White Sects and Black Men in the Recent South. Nashville: Vanderbilt University Press, 1971.

James, William. "The Perception of Reality," The Principles of Psychology. 2 vols., New York: Henry Holt and Co., 1890, II, ch. 21.

Janeway, Elizabeth. Man's World, Woman's Place: A Study in Social Mythology. New York: William Morrow, 1971.

Jenkins, William Sumner. Pro-Slavery Thought in the Old South. Chapel Hill: University of North Carolina Press, 1935.

Jordan, Winthrop D. White over Black: American Attitudes toward the Negro 1550-1812. 1968; Baltimore: Penguin Books, 1969.

Kovel, Joel. White Racism: A Psychohistory. New York: Random House Vintage Books, 1971.

Laslett, Peter. The World We Have Lost: England before the Industrial Age. 2nd ed. New York: Scribner's, 1973.

Lévi-Strauss, Claude. Structural Anthropology. 1958; New York: Basic Books, 1963.

McLean, Robert Colin. George Tucker: Moral Philosopher and Man of Letters. Chapel Hill: University of North Carolina Press, 1961.

McWilliams, Wilson Carey. The Idea of Fraternity in America. Berkeley: University of California Press, 1973.

Miller, Perry. Errand into the Wilderness. New York: Harper Torchbooks, 1956.

Morgan, Edmund S. American Slavery American Freedom: The Ordeal of Colonial Virginia. New York: W. W. Norton, 1975.

Mullin, Gerald W. Flight and Rebellion: Slave Resistance in Eighteenth-Century Virginia. New York: Oxford University Press, 1972.

Myrdal, Gunnar. An American Dilemma: The Negro Problem and Modern Democracy. 2 vols., New York: Harper & Brothers, 1944.

Newby, I. A. Jim Crow's Defense: Anti-Negro Thought in America, 1900-1930. Baton Rouge: Louisiana State University Press, 1965.

Niebuhr, Helmut Richard. The Kingdom of God in America. 1937; New York: Harper Torchbooks, 1959.

Niebuhr, Reinhold. "The Truth in Myths," The Nature of Religious Experience: Essays in Honor of Douglas Clyde Macintosh. Ed. Julius S. Bixler, R. L. Calhoun, and H. R. Niebuhr, New York: Harper & Brothers, 1937.

Posey, Walter Brownlow. The Baptist Church in the Lower Mississippi Valley 1776-1845. Lexington: University of Kentucky Press, 1957.

________. The Development of Methodism in the Old Southwest, 1783-1824. Tuscaloosa, Ala.: Weatherford Printing Co., 1933.

________. Frontier Mission: A History of Religion West of the Southern Appalachians to 1861. Lexington: University of Kentucky Press, 1966.

________. The Presbyterian Church in the Old Southwest, 1778-1838. Richmond: John Knox Press, 1952.

Ricoeur, Paul. The Symbolism of Evil. 1967; Boston: Beacon Press, 1969.

Robert, Joseph Clarke. The Road from Monticello: A Study of the Virginia Slavery Debate of 1832. 1941; rpt. New York: AMS Press, 1970.

Rossiter, Clinton. Conservatism in America: The Thankless Persuasion. 2nd ed. 1962; New York: Alfred A. Knopf, 1966.

Schochet, Gordon J. Patriarchalism in Political Thought: The Authoritarian Family and Political Speculation and Attitudes Especially in Seventeenth-Century England. New York: Basic Books, 1975.

Smith, Hilrie Shelton. In His Image but ...; Racism in Southern Religion, 1780-1910. Durham, N.C.: Duke University Press, 1972.

Smith, Timothy L. Revivalism and Social Reform: American Protestantism on the Eve of the Civil War. 1957; New York: Harper Torchbooks, 1965.

Stampp, Kenneth M. The Peculiar Institution: Slavery in the Ante-Bellum South. 1956; New York: Alfred A. Knopf, 1968.

Stanton, William. The Leopard's Spots: Scientific Attitudes toward Race in America 1815-1859. Chicago: University of Chicago Press, 1960.

Sydnor, Charles S. The Development of Southern Sectionalism 1819-1848. Vol. V of A History of the South, ed. W. H. Stephenson and E. M. Coulter. Baton Rouge: Louisiana State University Press, 1948.

U.S. Bureau of the Census. The Statistical History of the United States from Colonial Times to the Present. Stamford, Conn.: Fairfield Publishers, 1965.

Voegelin, Eric. The Ecumenic Age. Vol. IV of Order and History. Baton Rouge: Louisiana State University Press, 1974.

Whitfield, Theodore M. Slavery Agitation in Virginia 1829-1832. Baltimore: Johns Hopkins Press, 1930.

Wilmore, Gayraud S. Black Religion and Black Radicalism. New York: Doubleday, 1972.

Woodward, Comer Vann. American Counterpoint: Slavery and Racism in the North-South Dialogue. Boston: Little, Brown, 1971.

## Index


Abolitionists 2, 5, 15, 18-23, 34-35, 38, 44, 47, 51, 66, 68, 92, 111
Agassiz, Louis 24-25
Allen, Richard 96
American Anti-Slavery Society 2
American School of Ethnology see Polygenesis
Antislavery societies 2, 35
Arkansas 35

Bachman, John 75, 102
Baldwin, Samuel Davies 20, 23, 92, 96-98, 100-101, 103, 125-126
Baptists 17-18, 20, 40, 105
Barnes, Albert 16, 22
Berger, Peter 132-133
Bible: and antislavery 5-7, 21-23, 47; attacks against 15, 24-25, 70; and conservative political theory 39-41, 59 n. 26, 111-114; and constitutional theory 7, 18, 20-24, 112; and proslavery 3-7, 20-23, 111-114
Blyden, Edward 47, 96
Brookes, Iveson L. 73, 103
Brown, John 78
Brownlow, William G. 103
Bunyan, John 129
Byrd, William, II 50

Caldwell, David 19
Calhoun, John C. 19, 21, 37-41, 56, 65
Calmet, Augustin 43-44, 73
Capitalism, Southern critique of 54-56, 113
Carey, Lott 96
Cartwright, Samuel A. 72-73, 75-76, 83-84, 98-100, 103, 105, 124, 126, 130, 134
Catholics 18, 105
Channing, William Ellery 23
Charleston, S.C. 51
Clebsch, William A. xi-xiii, 14
Cobb, Howell 92, 103
Cobb, Thomas R. R. 21, 40, 46, 51-52, 76, 82-83
Cohen, Percy 126-127
Congregationalists 105
Conservative political theory 4, 37-41, 51, 58 n. 22, 59 n. 26, 114
Cooper, Thomas 15, 19
Cortés, Hernando 128
Cotton 35-36, 51
Crawford, William H. 19
Crummel, Alexander 96

Dabney, Robert Lewis 21-23, 102, 134
Dagg, John Leadley 20, 40, 42, 103
Dalcho, Frederick 78, 103

DeBow, James D. B. 3, 12, 15, 24-25, 129
Declaration of Independence 2, 34, 38, 66
Delany, Martin 96
Deslondes, Charles 58 n.15
Dew, Thomas R. 2-4, 32, 36-37, 45, 68-69, 71
Douglass, Frederick 16, 52, 68, 83-84

Eliade, Mircea 126
England, John 42, 103
Episcopalians 18, 105
Estes, Matthew 77, 103
Explorers in Africa 67, 76

Filmer, Robert 49-50
Fitzhugh, George 15, 32, 45, 54-56, 73, 109, 120
Fletcher, John 22, 78, 103
Fourier, Charles 55
Fredrickson, George M. 66

Garnet, Henry Highland 96
Garrison, William Lloyd 2, 68
Geertz, Clifford 1, 8, 110-111, 113, 117, 128
Genovese, Eugene 52, 80
Georgia 18, 33, 36-37
German Reformed 105
Gilbert (ringleader in Gabriel Prosser's revolt) 52
Gliddon, George 24-25, 105
Greenberg, Kenneth 38, 51

Hamilton, William T. 25
Hammond, James H. 15-16, 21, 56
Harper, William 21
Harrell, David 138
Helper, Hinton Rowen 66
Hemp 51
Holly, James T. 96
Hunter, Robert M. T. 54

Indentured servants 33
Indigo 33

Janeway, Elizabeth 131
Jefferson, Thomas 14-15, 33-34, 38, 67, 69, 71, 75
Johnson, Reverdy 103
Jordan, Winthrop 33, 67, 70

Kentucky 18, 35
Ker, Leander 48-49, 74, 103

Laslett, Peter 49-50
Legare, Hugh S. 19
Lévi-Strauss, Claude 117, 126
Liberia 2
Locke, John 38, 41, 49, 111
Lord, Nathan 103
Louisiana 18, 36
Lundy, Benjamin 35

McCaine, Alexander 20, 103
McDuffie, George 19
McWilliams, Wilson Carey 70
Malinowski, Bronislav 137
Manifest destiny 12-13, 23, 112-113; see also Myth of Ham and Japheth
Manigault, Louis 87
Marx, Karl 55
Maryland 33
Mell, Patrick H. 20, 75, 103
Methodists 16-18, 20, 40, 45, 105
Miller, Perry 12-13
Miscegenation 71, 77, 89 n.45
Mississippi 37
Missouri 18

Mitchell, J. C. 48, 103
Morgan, Edmund 32
Morton, Samuel G. 24, 75
Myrdal, Gunnar 137
Myth: definition of 123; function of 95, 109-110, 116-121, 133-134, 136-138; grammatical style of 123-126; as narrative 4, 117, 126-127; in a pluralistic society 105, 132-136; as symbolic framework for culture 7-8, 95, 100-102, 105, 117, 132; truth in 127-132
Myth of Ham and Japheth: and allegory 129-131; and the American Indian 7-8, 97-101; and biblical exegesis 5-7; and blackness 70-74; challenges to, by Southerners 102, 105; and the doctrine of original sin 42-44, 49; and the etymological arguments 42-44, 72-74; historical development of 43-44; as a legitimate myth 128-129, 135-136; and manifest destiny 5-8, 91-101; mediation by, to overcome contradictions of slavery 95, 109-110, 116-121; and patriarchalism 48-49, 84; popularity of, in the antebellum South 44-48, 101-105, 108; and the rabbinical tradition 44; and racism 70-74, 78-79, 84; reactions of black clergymen toward 7, 46-47, 96; and scientific arguments 72-73, 133-134; and stereotypes of blacks 44, 74, 78-79, 84, 101; structural analysis of 117-121

Newton, Thomas 43
Niebuhr, H. Richard 16, 18
North Carolina 18, 33, 35-36
Nott, Josiah 24-25, 70, 75

Original sin, the doctrine of: and conservative political theory 38-41; and proslavery argument 41-42, 109-112, 114-116; and inferiority of women 41, 60 n.32, 110

Patriarchal family 48-56, 82-84, 112-113; _see also_ Slavery and patriarchalism; Myth of Ham and Japheth and patriarchalism
Pennington, James W. C. 46-47
Petigru, James L. 19
Plantations: economic profitability of 33-37, 51, 113; number of slaves on 51; the rise of 32-33
Polygenesis 4, 12, 24-26, 65, 69-70, 75-76, 105, 109-111, 134
Presbyterians 17-20, 27, 40, 105
Priest, Josiah 42-43, 74, 78-79, 103, 105, 123-125
Proslavery argument: economic 33-36; social control of blacks 32, 34, 36-37; _see also_ Bible and proslavery; Racism and proslavery argument; Slavery, moral defense of

Prosser, Gabriel 52, 57 n.15
Providence of God, doctrine of 92-93, 112-113
Puritans 12-14, 18, 23, 49, 91-92, 112

Quakers 44, 66, 71

Racism: and blackness 70-74; and Christian orthodoxy 12, 69-70, 75, 80-82, 109-110, 114-116; and conservative political theory 4, 39, 114; and environmentalism 67-69, 115; and intelligence 75-78, 81-82; origin of 66-67, 70-71; and proslavery argument 65-84, 113; and science 4, 12, 65, 69-70, 75-77, 80-81; and sexual stereotypes 76-78, 81-82; see also Slavery and racism
Randolph, Thomas J. 34
Republican Party 66
Revivalism 14-20
Rice 33-36, 51
Rice, David 71
Rivera, Diego 128
Robinson, John Bell 49
Robinson, Solon 22, 53, 84, 103
Ross, Frederick A. 81, 96, 103

Saint Simon, Claude Henri de 55
Sawyer, George 83
Schaff, Philip 47-48, 95-96, 103
Sewall, Samuel 44
Shortridge, George D. 21
Simms, William Gilmore 1, 24, 69, 114-116
Slaves: abuse and suffering of 51-53, 77-78, 83-84; colonization of 2, 35, 37, 66, 94, 96; cost of 35-36, 57 n.12; discontent and revolts of 34, 36, 52, 57-58 n.15, 77-80, 83-84; manumission of 2, 35-37, 94, 96; marriages of 77; punishment of 33, 51-53, 83-84
Slavery: economic profitability of 2, 34-37, 66, 77, 113; inherent contradictions of 4, 51-53, 69-70, 79-80, 92, 115-116; moral defense of 1-3, 20, 32, 54, 113-114; origin of 33, 93; and patriarchalism 3, 51-53, 80, 82-84; and racism 66-72, 77-84, 114
Sloan, James A. 22, 41, 73, 103
Smith, Samuel Stanhope 67
Smith, Timothy 16
Smith, William 45
Smith, William A. 20, 40
Smyth, Thomas 25, 75, 81, 109-110
Socialism, a Southern critique of 55
South Carolina 18, 33, 36
Stampp, Kenneth 77
Stanton, William 69
Stephens, Alexander 20, 32, 45, 46
Stowe, Harriet Beecher 47, 51
Stringfellow, Thornton 5-6, 14, 20, 78, 82, 97, 101, 103, 130
Sugar 51
Sweet, William Warren 15
Sydnor, Charles S. 19, 34
Symbols, religious 1, 4-5 8, 116-117

Tennessee 35
Texas 35
Thornwell, James Henley 19
Thrasher, John B. 103
Tobacco 33-34, 51
Tucker, George 92, 104, 106 n. 4
Turner, Henry M. 96
Turner, Nat 34, 58 n. 15
Twain, Mark 46

Van Evrie, John H. 70-71, 75
Verot, Augustine 21-22, 81
Vesey, Denmark 58 n. 15
Virey, J. T. 76
Virginia 12-14, 18, 33-37, 49, 66-69
Virginia Company 32-33
Virginia legislature, debate before the (1831-1832) 2-3, 34-35, 66, 68
Voegelin, Eric 135-136

Waddel, Moses 19
Washington, George 33
Wayland, Francis 22
Weld, Theodore 5, 16, 47, 68
Wheat 34
Whitney, Eli 35
Wilmore, Gayraud S. 96
Woodward, C. Vann 49
Woolman, John 44, 71
Women, alleged inferiority of 41, 60 n. 32